HOW TO HAVE
AN
OBEDIENT DOG

Also available from Elliot Right Way Books

Choose & Bring Up Your Puppy
How To Have A Well-Mannered Dog

Uniform with this book

HOW TO HAVE AN OBEDIENT DOG

Jackie Marriott

RIGHT WAY

Typeset in 10/12pt Times by County Typesetters, Margate, Kent.
Printed and bound in Great Britain by Cox & Wyman Ltd., Reading, Berkshire.

The *Right Way* series and the *Paperfront* series are both published by Elliot Right Way Books, Brighton Road, Lower Kingswood, Tadworth, Surrey, KT20 6TD, U.K.

DEDICATION

To the first two dogs I owned during my adult life, Simon and Rupert, two little "terrors" who set me on the dog training road. Also, to my beloved Brumas, my first Bernese, who taught me, and gave me, so much.

THANKS

To my husband and fellow Dog Trainer, Vic, whose help and assistance has, as usual, been invaluable, and to Sandy Enzerink B.V.M.S. M.R.C.V.S. for checking the medical details and for her expertise in caring for my animals' health.

CONTENTS

LIST OF ILLUSTRATIONS

INTRODUCTION

Why Train Dogs?

The relationship between man and dog goes back many centuries, when man discovered that dogs were more efficient hunters than himself. Over a period of time he domesticated them to help him hunt, in return providing shelter and a share of the kill. It was a partnership from which both benefited. This, combined with the dog's social needs, i.e. a pack formation requiring a leader (man), led to the forming of bonds which have lasted to the present day.

Over the centuries, dogs have been used for a variety of tasks apart from hunting. These include retrieving game, herding sheep and other livestock, guard duties, guiding blind people and, more recently, as ears for the deaf. Dogs that were good at certain jobs were used for breeding and as a result the distinctive breeds developed.

Nowadays, large numbers of dogs are kept purely as pets and do not have any specific duties, other than being a companion. Those dogs which were developed for working, however, need to use and develop their basic instincts. Training can either encourage this, or, where the instincts are undesirable, channel them into activities which are acceptable in society. Training is essential for the big, strong breeds, but is also beneficial for smaller breeds, to improve nervousness or subdue aggression.

Well cared for, healthy dogs, are not carriers of disease nor are all dog lovers cranky or eccentric. However, because of the enormous amount of adverse criticism over recent years, owners need to train their dogs to be more socially acceptable.

Nobody likes dirty streets or dogs roaming in packs in urban areas. Nobody likes to hear about sheep being worried by dogs, or dogs left out to fend for themselves. Dogs, unlike people, have no morals; they do not know and abide by our codes of behaviour unless trained and supervised by a responsible owner. We cannot blame the errant dog, any more than we could blame a cat for following its natural instincts and killing a mouse, or a fox for killing a rabbit.

The methods used for training are basically very simple. We make as much use as possible of the natural instincts. As previously mentioned, dogs are pack animals in the wild, one dog being pack leader. This is usually the most powerful and intelligent dog. He may be challenged from time to time by subordinates and if a stronger dog wins the battle, the leader is replaced. In training dogs, we take over the role of pack leader, by inspiring respect, showing the dog we are superior to him, but also as soon as he complies with our wishes, he will receive affection and comfort.

1

PSYCHE OUT YOUR DOG!

Dog Logic

In an ideal world, before anyone acquired a dog, they would attend classes in canine psychology, study genetics, examine every breed for positive and negative traits and read all about the potential pitfalls of dog ownership. However, this is not an ideal world and the reasons why people get a dog are as varied as the breeds themselves.

The very best time to start training is whilst the dog is still a puppy, before he has a chance to learn any bad habits. Some of you reading this book may well be in that situation and you are the ones who should have the easiest job of all. Others may have had their dog for a few weeks or months and the problems have only just started to appear. Others still may have given a home to a "rescue" dog and perhaps, because of its previous home, the dog may have been allowed to develop many unacceptable habits, or have all kinds of phobias, both real and imaginary.

For all of you, the methods described in this book will enable you to have a happy, well adjusted and well controlled dog.

Before you start, it is as well to understand just how your dog "works". Much as you love him, you must accept that he is not blessed with human emotions, that he is an animal and a pack animal at that. By "pack", I mean that in his original and wild state, he was one of a group, with a leader, number two, number three, etc., in descending order. Where in the pack he stood depended on his character, physical strength and qualities of leadership.

Man has since domesticated the dog, but the very strong basic pack instinct remains and once the dog enters your family, he will look upon it as his "pack". It is entirely up to you who emerges as the leader – you, or the dog! If it is the dog, your family life could end up with the dog ruling everything, making your life and that of the rest of the family a misery. Perhaps you are already in that situation? If you are, or don't want that situation to develop, you must start now, setting yourself up as number one in the pack, with the rest of the family behind you and the dog at the bottom. I assure you that once he recognises you as "boss" and knows his place in the pack order, he will be a much happier animal.

As in all packs, there will be times when he will attempt to challenge your leadership and each challenge must be met in the same way – you are boss!

Priorities

Your dog has three basic priorities. Starting at the top, they are *food, affection* and *comfort*. Food being his most important, he will rarely, if ever, leave it for either of the other two. Comfort being the least important, he will happily leave lying down for a cuddle from you. He will quickly leave a cuddle if food is offered. You can demonstrate this with your own dog, to prove the point.

As far as training is concerned, it is not a good idea to use food as the primary inducement. Firstly, you will end up with a very fat dog and secondly you may not always have a tit-bit with you when you want your dog to comply with your wishes. So, for training purposes, you will be using his second priority – *affection* – and lots of it!

Correction

Throughout the book I will talk about correcting and rewarding your dog, so you have to know the right way to do both. Although I will go into correction first, do not, please, make the mistake of thinking that correction alone will train your dog – IT WON'T. All the correction in the world will be completely wasted unless you reward your dog properly.

By correction, I do not mean hitting your dog with sticks, leads, rolled-up newspapers, shoes; indeed hitting your dog with anything is counter-productive and can in some instances lead to your dog becoming aggressive. Apart from that, it is wasting a very valuable piece of training that your dog received long before you owned him.

As a new-born pup in the litter with his natural mother, he was taught from the moment of his birth what pleased his mum and what didn't. When he was naughty, she would grumble and growl, sometimes quite ferociously. Sometimes she would even nip him. Conversely, when he was being good, she would "stroke" him with her tongue and "cuddle" him, being very soft and gentle. She would allow him to play-fight with her, but never let him get the upper hand, always putting him in his place when the time was right.

If you get the chance, go and watch a bitch with her puppies. She can teach you more about dog behaviour than almost anyone else. Now, I'm not suggesting that you start biting your dog, but what you can do is to utilise that first basic training he learned from his Mum, and adapt it to fit. When your dog is displaying behaviour which is not acceptable to you, as his "replacement" parent, use your voice in a grumbly tone. Don't touch him in any pleasurable way. He will associate your actions and tone with the conditioning he received from his Mum and will understand that his actions have displeased you. (Also see page 100, *Mouthing and Play-Biting*.)

Reward

Rewarding your dog *should* be self-explanatory. Unfortunately, many owners find it difficult to convey genuine pleasure to their dog – a pat on the head and a verbal "good dog" is deemed to be appropriate. Others think that rewards should always be edible, with the end result being that the dog will only ever behave if food is offered.

Whenever your dog obeys you and pleases you, you must *show* him how happy you are with his compliance. Give him big enthusiastic cuddles. Stroke and touch him lovingly. Play with him. Tell him in an excited and happy voice that you are *delighted* with him.

Some people think a display of obvious affection towards their dog will adversely affect their position as number one in the "pack" order, or is somehow demeaning. Perhaps it has something to do with the traditional "British stiff upper lip"! They feel that such displays of affection will be interpreted by the dog as a sign of weakness. They may also feel they will lose control of the dog if they allow him to jump about and "go wild" for a few minutes.

Nothing could be further from reality. By showing your dog what pleases you, he will try much harder to please you in the future. As you will quickly have the ability to instil instant control when you say so, there is no danger that he will get the upper hand.

Try to imagine how you would feel if you had completed an exceptional job of work and no-one bothered to say "well done". It would hardly inspire you to work so hard again. Suppose there was no salary at the end of the month? I bet you wouldn't go back! Consider how you would feel if you had spent all day preparing a dinner party and not one of the guests said "thank you". Would you invite them back? Think of the dog's rewards in terms of his wages and signs of appreciation for a job well done. Reward every attempt, however small, that your dog makes to "get it right".

Boundaries

One of the earliest lessons your dog has to learn when he enters your family is where his boundaries are. By this, I mean what you are going to allow him to get away with. If you don't want him on the furniture, for example, then don't let him start. If he has already requisitioned a chair and you would rather he hadn't, then insist he removes himself, refusing to accept any show of aggression and praising him like mad when you succeed.

Don't make the mistake of treating him as you would a naughty child. There is an important difference between the two – a child has the ability to reason, a dog hasn't. You can explain to a naughty child why he is receiving punishment and he will understand. Dogs do not understand language and do not have the ability to reason, so any punishment or correction must be given *as he commits* the offence, otherwise he will not understand what the punishment is for.

I can almost hear you say "oh, but he knows when he's done wrong, he looks sad and runs away". No doubt he does know that you're angry, but I promise you that unless you actually caught him in the act, he does not and cannot know what has provoked your anger.

Let me give you an example. Suppose you have left the dog on his own and whilst you were out, he has chewed a big hole in the settee. You return home and your dog, thrilled to see you, comes rushing up to welcome you. You spot the ruined settee. With a face like thunder and a voice to match, you shout and scream at him, perhaps even hitting him. What have you taught him? You've taught him that when you come home, the best course of action for him to take is to run and keep well out of the way, as you're so cross when you come home. He has no way of knowing that his act of demolition, maybe done more than an hour before you returned, is the reason for your temper. How can he? He's forgotten all about it, the second he stopped chewing.

O.K. so what *should* you have done? In you come, dog rushes up to greet you. Having spotted the ruined settee, ignore it, cuddle your dog and let him welcome you home. Next, go up to the settee, *showing no sign of anger whatsoever.* Now encourage him to start chewing the settee! Sounds daft! No, because as he puts his teeth to it, that's when you correct him. Show him at that instant that what he's doing is wrong. He will immediately associate your anger with the action he is doing, i.e. chewing the settee. Apply this to anything he does which you dislike, i.e. digging holes in the garden, foraging in the rubbish bin, chewing your shoes etc., and he will instantly learn what is allowed and what isn't.

All the dog wants is to know where he stands and to be loved by you. All the time he is being good, love him to pieces. He will only want to do those things which get a favourable response from you and will not want to repeat any action which incurs your displeasure.

2

INFORMAL TRAINING

By informal training, I mean all those things which you want to teach your dog *not* to do, as opposed to formal training, which is teaching him things which you want him to do. Informal training can start from the moment he enters your house.

Possessiveness with Food

Having said earlier that food is his most important priority, an early and vital part of your establishing yourself as the leader is by showing him that he can only have his food at your discretion and command. Give him his dinner, let him eat for a few seconds, then take his bowl away from him. Use an appropriate sound each time you do so, such as **leave** or **stop**, and keep the bowl for a few seconds. Provided he did not show any sign of aggression as you removed the bowl, tell him "good boy", give it back and allow him to continue eating. Repeat this two or three times during each meal for a few days, then once or twice a week for a few weeks.

Any sign of aggression, however slight, must be corrected very firmly and immediately. Some dogs are never possessive with food, but you may find that if your dog came from a large litter, the way he obtained his share was by threatening his brothers and sisters. If such action achieved the desired result, i.e. getting more food, he may well try that with you. If you don't sort this out very early on, this possessiveness will transfer to other things, such as bones, toys, furniture and so on, perhaps even to members of the family.

And what happens if he has been allowed to get his most important priority, food, by showing aggression? Later, at any stage of his training which he doesn't want to comply with, he may attempt to repeat the aggressive action, which previously got him what he wanted.

Coming when Called – Early Training

Although this will be covered more fully in Chapter 3, you can start to formulate this exercise before ever putting a collar and lead on your dog. Food being the dog's first priority, use it to "condition" him to come when called.

Make sure he is in another part of the house whilst you prepare his dinner. When you are ready, have the bowl in your hands, holding it at chest height. Signal your dog to come, by calling his name and giving him the sound **come**, said with a very pleasant tone. His sense of smell will have already "told" him what is going on and he will no doubt come rushing to you. As he arrives at your feet, don't allow him to jump up for the bowl, but tell him to **sit**. Keep the bowl at chest height and do not give it to him yet. He will probably sit more than willingly; in fact at this stage he would probably walk across the ceiling if you told him to, such is his desire for food! Once he has sat, tell him to **wait** and place the bowl on the floor in front of him. Any attempt to get the bowl must be stopped; if necessary hold his "scruff" to restrain him. Make him wait at least five seconds, then tell him "go on then, good boy" and allow him to eat his food.

Now, quite easily and without any need for harsh correction, you have started the build-up to three separate exercises - coming when called – sit – wait – all of which

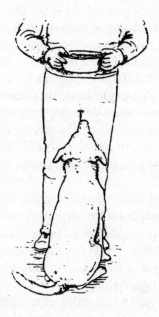

Fig. 1. Dinner is served!

you will be teaching formally later on. What you will have succeeded in doing is to start a very pleasant association in your dog's mind with returning to you when called to the sound of **come**, sitting when told to the sound of **sit** and waiting when told to the sound of **wait**, all being rewarded not only with a verbal sound from you, but with his dinner too!

Make sure that you give him the verbal reward clearly, plus some gentle stroking, as later on you won't be using his dinner bowl as a reward, so you want him to understand that praise is verbal as well as edible!

House Training

Although some of you will have progressed beyond this problem, I am including a section on it, firstly for those who have young puppies and secondly for those who are experiencing problems with a previously clean dog.

There are many different methods for teaching a dog to be clean and most people have their own "pet" theory. Like everything you want your dog to learn, you can teach him to be clean on command, by giving him a sound to go with the action! If you are having difficulties with house training, I suggest you start again from scratch and try my methods.

The "old wives tale" of rubbing the dog's nose in it is not only most unpleasant for all concerned and completely illogical, but more importantly it doesn't work. Likewise, it is no good "putting" your dog outside in the garden and hoping he will relieve himself. He may well do so, but he will not be learning anything.

Dogs need to go to the toilet at certain regular times, such as on waking, after a meal, after playing. Make sure that at all these times you immediately *take* him into the garden, staying out there with him, even if it is cold, wet and dark. As soon as he starts to relieve himself, give him a command to go with his action. I use "hurry up", but you can use any words you like, provided you keep them short.

Remember too, that you will eventually be giving him this same command when he is outside, with other people around, so do choose something sensible! Reward him profusely as he finishes, lots of "good dog, clever dog", etc.

If he always receives that praise when he relieves himself outside, he will quickly learn to associate the action with the reward. Any accidents indoors should be ignored. You may be able to stop him just before he squats, in which case quickly but *calmly* take him outside. Don't panic him, or he will forget what his original intention was.

With young puppies, you should take them outside at least once an hour to begin with. Again, with young puppies, you can start training them to paper if you prefer, although it does take a little longer to get them clean this way. Cover an area of the floor with the newspaper and take the puppy to it at all the relevant times, giving the same commands and praise as you will when he is outside. Over a few days, gradually reduce the area of paper, moving it slowly towards the back door. Move it progressively over the back doorstep and outside.

Make a point of putting the puppy on his lead sometimes when you take him out to be clean in the garden. He has to learn to relieve himself whilst being confined on a lead and some dogs get quite confused if previously they have only ever been running free when they want to relieve themselves. If you don't put them on the lead occasionally, it can take a long time to get the idea through to them that sometimes they have to remain on the lead and still go to the toilet.

GETTING CLEAN THROUGHOUT THE NIGHT. Getting the dog clean through the day is relatively easy, but the long period during the night can be a problem.

This could be for a variety of reasons. Sometimes, the young dog has simply not yet learnt to control himself and here you can try using the newspapers on the floor just for night-time use. It could be that he is "asking" to go out and has been unable to attract your attention. If this is the case, it may be worth setting your alarm clock a couple of times during the night, just for a week or two, so that you can let him out. Admittedly this will mean a broken night's sleep for you, but if the end justifies the means, so be it. Perhaps he has learned that if he stands by the back door, he is let into the garden, but of course at night-time nobody can see him as everyone's in bed.

It may be worth investing in a little D.I.Y. here, which can help solve the problem. Get a thin flat piece of hardboard and buy an ordinary battery-operated door-bell, complete with wire. Fix up the bell outside your bedroom door, running the wire to the back door, to floor. level. Attach the bell push towards the edge of the board and connect up the wire. Place the board, bell push side down, on the floor by the back door, if possible under the floor covering. When you put pressure on the board, the bell should ring. When your dog next goes to stand by the back door, asking to go out, he will stand on the board and hey presto! he will have operated the bell, alerting you that he wants to go outside. I have used this with several of my puppies, to great effect.

Sometimes it may just be a matter of altering his feeding times. If he is normally fed his last meal of the day around 6 p.m. his natural bodily functions will decree that he will want to relieve himself at about 3 a.m. Try either bringing his last meal forward, or leaving it until much later. Also, to ensure that his bladder is empty before he goes to bed, pick up the water bowl at 5 p.m. Obviously, if he has been playing energetically, allow access to the water for a short while to satisfy his thirst, then remove it again.

ONLY GOING TO THE TOILET IN THEIR GARDEN. There are some dogs who, having grasped the idea of going to the toilet in the garden, seem to think that it is the *only* place they can go. You take them out for a walk, but they "hang on" until they return home. Maturity usually tends to solve this particular snag, but in the meantime it can be quite a problem, especially if you are taking the dog out for the day, or going away on holiday. You must persevere with the training, encouraging him all the time he is outside, giving him the command he has learnt in the garden.

If necessary, stop him going into the garden at all for a few days. On every occasion when he normally wants to go to the toilet, put him on his lead and take him out to the park or wherever, giving him his command and, eventually, nature should take over! This may be time-consuming but it will pay dividends in the end.

In view of the enormous amount of publicity which has been given to the problem of dogs fouling public areas, it can sometimes be a positive advantage if your dog prefers his own back garden! Do try and be a thoughtful dog owner when you are out exercising your dog. No-one, dog owner or non-dog owner, likes stepping in dog excreta, so always take a few plastic bags with you so that you can clear up after your dog. Plastic bags are not cumbersome and are very simple to use. Just place your hand inside the bag, scoop up the "deposit", turn the bag inside out using your other hand, seal it and place it in the nearest litter bin. Your hand will not come into contact with anything unpleasant and your dog will not be causing any offence by leaving little "presents" behind him!

ACCIDENTS CAUSED BY EXCITEMENT. This seems to be more common with young animals and usually affects bitches more than males. Usually the dog doesn't want or intend to be dirty, but gets so excited that he simply cannot help himself. First of all, DO NOT PUNISH THE DOG, you will only make matters worse, as the dog will become so nervous of your reaction that he will relieve himself through fear. To try and overcome the situation, be very calm when you first greet your dog – not cool, but controlled, and immediately go through to the garden with the dog, where you can greet him properly and any "accident" will not matter.

Usually they grow out of this problem, but if it persists, it may be something physical and a trip to the vet may be necessary.

HABITUALLY DIRTY DOGS. With some dogs it becomes a habit to urinate and defecate wherever they choose. It may be that they have never been properly house trained, or because they have a very strong territorial instinct and feel the need to mark out their territory.

In the first case, where the dog has simply been allowed to become dirty, you must go right back to the basic training, as you would for a young puppy. If he is a "territory marker", he may be urinating on the furniture, especially in a strange house. Obviously, if you can catch him "in the act", a quick correction may save the day – and the sofa! It doesn't seem to make any difference even if the dog has just relieved himself outside – the instinct to leave his mark is so strong. If the problem only occurs when you take him to strange houses, the only answer may be not to take the dog in.

If the problem is happening in the dog's own home, then try moving the furniture, as often dogs tend to do it in the same spot and by putting a piece of furniture on that spot, you may break the habit. There are products you can buy which have a smell and taste repugnant to the dog. Sprayed over the relevant area this may help to stop the dog dirtying that spot.

There is a theory that with male dogs who urinate indoors, having them castrated can be the answer. It does work sometimes, but castration is *not* the answer to every training problem, as some people tend to think. It most certainly should not be contemplated until the dog is completely mature and then only after discussing it thoroughly with your vet.

There is now available a course of injections which can simulate temporarily the result of castration and is worth considering before you have your dog operated on. If the injections work, there is a good chance that the castration will too, but if they don't work, the chances of castration working are remote. In Chapter 5, page 117, I go into the advantages and disadvantages of both castrating male dogs and spaying the females, so please read as much as possible about the likely outcome of such operations, before you take such a step.

BACKWARD STEPS. It is quite common for dogs who have previously "got the idea" of being clean to revert to being dirty again, usually when they are around four-to-five months old. This generally coincides with them starting to teethe and is only a passing phase. Understanding and patience are required and a few days' repetition of initial house training will usually sort the problem out.

Likewise, some bitches become dirty indoors just before they start their season. It is basically because their hormones are "having a sort out" and is only temporary, so do be patient. Emotional upset within the family, moving house, or indeed any change in the normal routine can get the dog's "wires" crossed temporarily. This especially applies to "rescue" dogs, who may have undergone quite an emotional trauma and are having difficulty adjusting to a new home and new routine. Do be really patient, treat the dog as you would a young puppy and the problem will soon be solved.

Routine

Because any upset in routine can cause possible problems with house training, it is important that you establish early on a regular routine for your dog. All the important things in his life should happen in a regular pattern, such as eating, walking and sleeping, allowing his head and his body to get into a "system". Imagine the effect on his stomach if you fed him at 8 a.m. on one day and at 2 p.m. the next. His stomach would soon get very upset, as would his sleeping and toilet routine.

The same thing happens if there is no regularity in his life and no consistency over what he is and is not allowed to do. He can only adapt into the human way of life if he has a regular timetable, i.e. feeding, sleeping, exercise, playing, being left, etc. Even though it is not ideal for you to leave your dog all day whilst you go to work, he can adjust to long periods of being alone – although of course you will have to make sure that the time he does spend with you is as full and interesting as possible.

As well as the routine of the household, you should get him into a regular routine of being brushed and "looked at". Examining your dog may sound strange, but if you get him used to his ears being checked, his teeth, eyes, feet, etc., all being held and examined, it will make your job, and that of the vet, much easier when the dog is unwell and in need of attention. It is very difficult, for example, to bandage up a cut paw when the dog won't let you near his feet!

Get used to the look and feel of him when he is healthy, so that you will quickly be able to spot when something is wrong. For those of you who have a female dog, make sure you know what her intimate parts look like, so that you will be able to see the difference when she starts her season. If you don't know how to tell when she is in season, by the time you do notice, it may be too late – she may already be pregnant!

Leaving the Dog Alone

At some stage, you are going to have to leave your dog alone, whether it is to go to work, or just to the shops. If you have first taught him that being left is part of his routine and there are times when he can't come with you, he will soon accept the situation. Don't just go out and expect him to behave, teach him first what you expect.

Decide where you are going to leave him, either confined in one room, or in the garden, or with the run of the house. Make sure that there is nothing lying around on which he could hurt himself, or which is accessible for chewing. If you are leaving him in the garden, obviously make sure it is totally secure.

When you have decided on an area, arrange a practice session by pretending to go out. Do all the things that you normally do when you really go out, such as collecting up your bag, putting your coat on, shutting doors, etc. Begin by teaching him an association with a set of sounds which he will learn mean that he is to remain at home, you are going out, but you *are* coming back. I usually say "just going over the road, won't be long" every time I leave my dogs, whether I'm going out for ten minutes or a couple of hours. They now associate those sounds with me going, then a period of being left alone, then me coming back, as I have done every time after I have given them those sounds.

So, decide on what you're going to say, say it and leave the house. Stand outside the door, very quietly. Any sound of barking, scratching, whining, etc., must be dealt with *instantly*. Rush back indoors, grumble and say "Bad dog", enforcing your displeasure with a shake if necessary. Don't touch him or speak to him in any pleasant way at all, but don't shout and scream at him either. Immediately you have chastised him, leave him again. Only when he has been quiet for five minutes do you go back in, this time full of love and praise, thus teaching him that being quiet gets a lovely reaction, i.e. loads of affection, whereas to disturb the peace provokes a most unpleasant reaction from you. Slowly, over a period of several days, increase the length of time you leave him, until he has been quiet for half an hour without your having to correct him. Then you can start going out properly for short periods of time, gradually increasing the amount so that you can eventually trust the dog to be left for as long as necessary within your household routine.

HOWLING AND CHEWING. Sometimes the silence of an empty house can distress the dog and may start him howling or barking. Sometimes, because of the silence, dogs can hear noises outside more easily, thereby provoking them into barking. Try leaving the radio on when you go out, as the sound of human voices may soothe the distressed dog and mask the external sounds for the barking dog. Some dogs learn to be very destructive when they are left alone and young puppies, particularly, like to chew, especially when they are losing their baby teeth. In this instance, leave them something they *can* chew which is not going to matter. I have found that a pile of empty cardboard boxes, the sort you can get from the supermarket, provide a dog with endless amusement, as they can demolish them beautifully! Of course, you must remove any staples or wire first.

By leaving the boxes for him to chew, you are getting two distinct benefits. Firstly, he is not damaging the furniture or the carpets and all you have to clear up when you return are pieces of cardboard. Secondly, you will not inadvertently be teaching him to chew anything precious, as you would if you gave him an old slipper or shoe to play with. If you do actually give him an old shoe to demolish, you can hardly be surprised when he chews up your best pair – how is he supposed to know the difference between old ones and new ones?

For puppies who are teething, I have found that an old saucepan or frying pan comes in useful – and no, not for hitting him with! When he's teething, he wants something cold and hard with which he can ease his painful gums, so you can see that such an article is ideal. Obviously, make sure there are no sharp edges or loose screws on which he could harm himself and don't use the non-stick variety, as this could poison him. One word of warning here – if they try to carry it around in their mouths, watch out for your shins, as a clout from a metal pan really hurts – and I speak from very painful experience!

Dogs who Steal

It is quite natural for a dog to take things in his mouth – after all, he doesn't have hands! Unfortunately, it is often the owners who inadvertently teach their dogs to steal. A fairly typical reaction to seeing your dog wandering around with your best pair of socks in his mouth, is to chase after him and shout at him to leave them. He runs away and it turns firstly into a game and secondly into a way of challenging your authority and getting you to lose your temper. This all culminates in him stealing at every opportunity.

What you *should* do is to encourage him to bring whatever he has in his mouth to you, by praising him and telling him what a clever dog he is, saying "good boy, come and bring it here". When he does come up, all pleased with himself, reward him and tell him to **give**, holding your hands level with his mouth and taking the article as he opens his mouth. As you are going to be ever so nice when he brings it to you, he will enjoy your reaction so much that he will not want to run away. He may even end up actively seeking things out to bring to you.

You will probably end up with the sofa piled high with

socks, clothes, shoes, slippers, shopping bags, etc., but at least they will not have been hidden or destroyed. He will have learned a valuable lesson in what pleases you, plus you will have the added bonus of laying down the groundwork for the retrieve exercise. Retrieving is not necessary for the average pet to learn, but if you want to do obedience competitively later on, you will have already done some basic training towards it.

Jumping up

Why do dogs jump up? Usually because they are pleased to see you and jumping up gets them closer to you, especially your face. Think about your reaction when the dog jumps. You probably touch him with your hands to push him off. Or to "get it over with", you stroke him, say "hello" and are generally pleasant.

Either way, as far as he is concerned his action of jumping has received a favourable response from you, i.e. you have touched him and spoken to him. So he will repeat the action which gave him that response – he will jump up again.

So, how do you stop it? Initially, you will need to enlist the help of a friend, who is going to be a very silent assistant. Put the dog on his lead and get your friend to hold him. You then go out of the front door, wait a few minutes then come back in. Your assistant is not going to restrain the dog from coming to greet you; he will simply be holding the end of the lead at this stage.

As the dog launches himself at you, keep your hands well away from him. Give him the verbal command **off**, at the same time bringing your knee up to deflect the dog. Simultaneous with your command of **off** your assistant will jerk the lead downwards, putting pressure on the collar and causing the dog to return to the floor, quicker than he would do naturally. Any attempt to jump up again must be corrected in exactly the same way. Once the dog has all four feet on the ground, go down to his level and reward him lavishly, stroking him and telling him what a good dog he is.

Remember, your helper must remain silent, only being there to enforce your verbal command. Repeat the exercise until your dog makes no attempt to jump at you when you come in the door, not forgetting to reward him every time.

You can then change the situation around, with you holding the lead and your friend coming in the door, who will do exactly as you have done previously.

You may think that once the lead is removed, the dog will start leaping up again, but if the timing of you and your assistant is correct, the dog will associate the sound of the command with the extra, uncomfortable correction provided by the lead. After a few sessions of practice, you will find that the verbal command is quite enough. Very soon he will make no attempt to jump up, as he will have learnt that the quickest way to get you to touch and speak to him is by remaining on the floor, whereas jumping up does not get the reaction he wants.

Finally, please do not use the word **down** for this exercise. This word is going to mean something completely different during later training and you do not want to confuse the dog. Each sound is to mean one thing and one thing only.

Barking

The dog which barks unnecessarily is a pain to live with and agony to live next door to! Some dogs bark because their guarding instinct is very strong and they feel it necessary to alert you to every little noise. Some bark because they are nervous and the sound of their own barking gives them confidence. Some bark because they like the reaction it provokes in you and some bark simply because they haven't been taught not to. It is quite normal for a dog to bark if someone comes to the door or if he hears a strange noise during the night. Continuing to bark after an acceptable time is what you want to deter.

In most cases, the way to stop a dog barking is to teach him to bark on command! This may sound very strange, but it does work. At the same time as teaching him to bark, you are also teaching him when *not* to bark.

For the dog to learn this exercise, you again need to enlist the help of a friend, so that you can set up the situation. You should be sitting relaxing, then your helper, at a pre-arranged time, should come to the door and ring the bell. Your dog will then naturally bark and as he does so, give him the command **speak**. Allow him to bark for five seconds, then command him **quiet**, giving him lots of fuss when he does. Don't attempt to answer the door until the dog is silent. Then go to the door, open it, speak to your friend on the doorstep, as you would a casual caller, then close the door.

Go back and sit down again and after an interval of about ten minutes, repeat the whole process again. Alternate between talking to your friend on the doorstep and inviting him in, to simulate what would sometimes happen, i.e. someone coming to the door, then being invited into the house.

Try to repeat this over a few days, building up the association with the dog that he is allowed to bark for just a few seconds when that doorbell rings, but he must stop when you say so, the door never being opened until he has stopped barking. You are also getting him to associate the sound of your command **speak** with his barking.

Why must the door *never* be opened until he is silent? If you allow him to continue to bark whilst you open the door, he will associate that it is his action of barking which gets the door open, resulting in future problems. If he is the type of dog who imagines there is someone at the door and barks often unnecessarily, the only way you will get him to be quiet is to go and open it. You may even end up in a situation of the dog training you – every time he wants attention, he will bark to provoke you into getting up to answer the door to an imaginary caller.

Having taught him to bark on the command **speak**, you will then be able to get him to bark if ever you feel in a threatening situation – when you're out for a walk, perhaps, and are approached by a suspicious character, or if you should hear a strange noise in the middle of the night. You can also apply the same training if your dog barks every time the telephone rings. Arrange for a friend to telephone you and don't answer until the dog is quiet. On these occasions though, don't practise by giving him the **speak** command, as you don't want him barking every time the phone rings. Simply correct him for barking unnecessarily at the telephone.

DOGS WHO BARK BECAUSE THEY LIKE THE REACTION IT PROVOKES: Sometimes it is your action in response to the dog barking which can actually make the situation worse. In an attempt to shut the dog up quickly, you tend to rush to answer the door or the telephone and in the process get the dog even more excited. If you think you may be guilty of this, then deliberately do not answer the door, etc., having previously arranged with a friend either to telephone or ring your doorbell. If you show no sign of agitation with the ringing noise, you will take the excitement out of the situation.

You may have fallen into the trap of shouting at the dog each time he barks – or even taken to chasing after him to get him to be quiet. As far as he is concerned, the whole thing turns into a game, at the same time he has learned how to provoke you and get you to lose your temper, thus challenging your authority as pack leader.

He may be the type of dog who simply stands in the garden, head thrown back, barking like crazy and waiting for some reaction from you. If you recognise this situation, indulge in what I call "negative" training. As it is your reaction which excites and stimulates him, you are going to show no reaction whatsoever. It isn't easy to ignore a barking dog, but you need to give an Oscar-winning performance of complete indifference! Don't speak to him, don't look at him, read the newspaper, pretend to be asleep, show no reaction *at all*. The dog will then probably become curious as to your lack of interest and will come over to you enquiringly. When he does, give him a calm, gentle pat, tell him "good dog", etc., and carry on reading. As far as he is concerned, it's no fun if he can't get you to react, so he will shut up.

After a few minutes of silence, make a point of going over to him and fuss and play with him. You are thereby conditioning the dog that noise gets no reaction from you, but when he is silent he gets the attention he wants.

THE NERVOUS, HYSTERICAL BARKER. If you have the type of dog who rushes out into the garden, barking at unseen terrors, or simply rushes out barking because he likes the sound of his own voice, shock tactics can sometimes work.

Have ready a plastic jug filled with cold water. When he starts his ear-splitting routine, sidle up to him very casually and throw the water over his head. Don't speak as you do it, but praise him like mad the second he stops. Better still, if you can arrange to "bomb" him with the water from an upstairs window, or from an unobserved position, without him realising where the water has come from, it can be far more effective. Once again, he will have received a most unpleasant reaction to his barking, which should prove quite a deterrent in the future.

This method can also be applied if you have a dog who barks whilst travelling in the car. Substitute for the jug a water pistol or plant spray. When the barking starts, aim the jet of the spray between his eyes, again saying nothing as you do it, but praising like mad when he stops. It is obviously much safer if someone else is driving the car at the time!

Car Travel and Travel Sickness

Many dogs develop a fear of car travel and become sick during the journey. Unfortunately we as dog owners inadvertently contribute towards this.

Usually the very first experience a dog has with a car is when you collect him from the place where he was bred. The trauma of leaving his mum, brothers and sisters, plus the people he has become used to, is compounded by being put into a moving machine, possibly for several hours. The car thus becomes an upsetting place, associated with being taken away from his first family.

Then, he settles in with you and more than likely his very next trip in the car is to the vet for a check-up and his first inoculations, again compounding his opinion that cars are most unpleasant places to be, this time associated with having an injection. The car has turned into a monster and his dislike of it increases. Fortunately, most dogs do grow out of this phobia as they mature, but some retain their hatred.

There are various things which you can do to help him overcome this fear and reinstate the car as a place of pleasure. Use his highest priority, food, and start to give him one of his daily meals in the car, whilst it is parked outside your home. His love of food should overcome any reluctance to enter the car, coupled with lots of encouraging sounds from you.

When you have done this for a few days, set aside half an hour, when you can take your dog to the car and sit in there with him, again whilst the car is stationary. Turn the radio on, talk calmly and lovingly to him all the time. When you've done this a few times, start the engine, letting it run for a few minutes, still talking all the time to the dog. Don't try and rush any stage.

When he seems calm being in the car while it is stationary, yet with the engine running, plan a short trip, either to the park (assuming he has had all his inoculations), or to visit someone whom the dog is fond of. Slowly, build up the association that nice things happen when he is in the car, gradually increasing the time spent in the car and the distance travelled.

If he is prone to being sick, make sure that he travels with an empty stomach. For the very nervous dog, the type who tries to charge around in the car, restrain him by attaching his lead to a strong bracket inside the car, putting him in the down position. Leave him enough room so that he can turn his head, but not so much that he can sit up and move about.

Dogs who will not remain still are not only very dangerous in a car, but the tearing about only succeeds in winding them up further. In very extreme cases you can obtain tranquillisers from the vet, but try not to rely on these permanently.

Strange Sights and Sounds

As soon as you bring a new puppy into your home, start accustoming him to as many different sights and sounds as possible. This applies equally to older dogs as well, which you have given a home to, as you have no way of knowing what might frighten them. Get them used to all the usual domestic noises, such as the washing machine, vacuum cleaner, hair dryer, etc. Deal with any show of fear as it arises, being very calm, patient and loving. As soon as the dog has had all his inoculations, make a point of taking him along roads which have heavy traffic, accustom him to pedestrian crossings, level crossings, etc. Take him across pedestrian bridges and under pedestrian subways. If he shows apprehension at any of these things, don't avoid them, but make a point of taking him to them regularly. For example, if he is showing fear of heavy traffic, take the time to stand on the pavement with him – obviously well back from the edge of the road – talk calmly to him all the time, stroke him and if necessary, give him the odd tit-bit. Don't baby him, or try and avoid taking him past any of his "terrors". You will only make matters worse. If you are too sympathetic, it will only convince him that there really is something to be frightened of. He needs to get his confidence from you, so adopt a gentle but chivying attitude, be kind, lots of fuss, but don't try to protect him.

If your puppy is still small, don't be tempted to pick him up. Apart from not curing his fear, you could be setting up a situation when he will ask to be carried – easy enough when he only weighs a few pounds, but a full grown labrador or similar is not so easy to pick up! Likewise, if you have a small dog, which is easy to carry, please don't. However tiny they may be, they are *dogs*, and as such should be treated like dogs, not children.

Make a point of taking the dog to crowded, noisy places. An ideal venue to socialise your dog is the local pub. The combination of crowds of people, juke boxes and fruit machines will all help to make him completely bomb-proof. Of course, another advantage of taking him to the pub is that it gives you a perfect excuse for "popping down to the local"! Don't forget to take the dog though!

Getting your Dog used to Children

If you have children in your family, make sure they understand that the dog is *not* a toy. Most dogs brought up with children are incredibly tolerant towards them and will put up with treatment that they would never accept from an adult. Provide the dog with a place of safety to which he can retreat when he's had enough. If all the children understand that when the dog takes himself off to his basket, for example, he is to be left alone, the dog will willingly put up with all kinds of things, as he knows he can escape whenever he wishes. Don't let the children torment or degrade the dog, however tolerant he may be. They must be taught to respect the dog, in the same way that the dog must respect them.

If you haven't any children at home, get the dog used to other people's children as soon as possible. Dogs who are nervous or aggressive towards children can be quite a handicap. Children can be quite unkind to dogs, prodding and poking them, shouting and rushing about, so make sure that the children to whom you introduce your dog have themselves been properly trained! At the first meeting, use food as an inducement and have the child give the dog a tit-bit, thereby giving a pleasant association to the dog in connection with children.

Finally, however well behaved your dog is around children, it is most unwise to leave a dog alone with young children. Anything could happen, from the children letting the dog out onto the road, to their provoking the dog so much that he ends up biting them. The dog cannot speak and his only answer to cruel treatment, however unintentional it may be, is to use his teeth.

Young babies especially should never be left alone with any dog. As far as the dog is concerned, babies make funny noises and smell very interesting, arousing his basic natural instincts and curiosity, which could have disastrous consequences. Having said that, don't immediately get rid of the dog if a new baby comes along. Just be sensible and vigilant and the two of them will happily coexist.

Dog Training Clubs

As soon as your puppy is old enough, join a dog training club. More and more clubs are coming around to the opinion that the earlier a puppy starts his training the better and will let you join as soon as the puppy has had all his inoculations. As well as the advantage of getting help with training problems, it is an excellent way of socialising your dog with people and other dogs.

Clubs usually advertise in the local paper, library and vets' waiting rooms. Go along and watch a couple of times before joining, to assess whether it is the right club for you. Are the instructors continually telling the members to praise their dogs? Are they explaining *why* the dogs do certain things, as well as how to deal with each problem? Are the dogs working happily, tails wagging? If so, these are all good indications that the instruction and training is on the right lines. Talk to the other members, find out about the social aspect of belonging to the club. Use your common sense and you will soon work out whether it's a good club.

Dogs who Eat their Droppings

Almost without exception, when a dog eats his own waste matter, or indeed that of another animal, the owner is appalled and revolted, thinking perhaps that they have a perverted dog on their hands.

The correct term for this practice is coprophagia and it is quite common, not only amongst dogs but many other animals as well. Young puppies often exhibit this behaviour, much to the distress of their owners. A bitch with her litter naturally cleans up after her pups, but this does not mean she is always going to do it, even after her pups have gone to their new homes.

Coprophagia is usually a behavioural problem, but I would always advise owners to take their dogs for a check-up at the vet's first, to ensure that there is no physiological reason why the dog is doing this, especially so in the case of an adult dog who suddenly starts. There are various medical reasons for this behaviour. They are: vitamin or mineral deficiency/pancreatic insufficiency/malnutrition/a low roughage diet/parasitic burden/hyperthyroidism.

Obviously, if the cause is medical, then treatment will cure the problem. If no medical reason is found, then corrective training should help resolve the problem. You approach this in the same way that you would teach him not to chew the furniture, dig holes in the garden, demolish slippers, etc. Showing no anger at all, you put him in his training collar and lead, take him up to the droppings and encourage him to attempt to eat them (I know it's unpleasant). As he goes to eat them, correct him, both with the collar and verbally, saying firmly **no** or **leave**, rewarding him each time he refrains. Repeat this several times until he shows no interest whatsoever in eating the droppings, remembering to reward him profusely for his compliance.

Sometimes, dogs start eating their droppings simply out of boredom, particularly if the dog is left alone for long periods of time. Breaking the boredom will often break the habit. Try to rearrange your schedule so that the time he is left is reduced. If that is not possible, ask if a neighbour or friend could pop in to see the dog, breaking up the time span of being alone. Leave him harmless things to play with, not slippers or rubber balls, but empty cardboard boxes which he can demolish.

Another canine companion would obviously be an

answer, but it is hardly fair on another dog, just getting him as companionship for the first one. The second dog will require attention and training and if you are away from the house for long periods of time, he is not going to get the consideration from you that he deserves. A cat can sometimes provide company for a lonely dog, but a cat is not generally a social animal and will more than likely go off and do his own thing, leaving the dog alone again. Really, the only answer is not to leave the dog for so long in the first place.

Obviously, if the dog is eating his own droppings, then clearing them up as soon as they are deposited will prevent it.

Rolling

Rolling in animal droppings, or indeed other foul smelling substances, is another example of how our dogs unwittingly offend us. We think of it as dirty, disgusting behaviour. To a dog though, it is a normal, instinctive part of his canine personality.

One of the most commonly accepted reasons for this behaviour is that, in dog language, the stronger and more pungent he smells, the more superior he appears to another dog. This desire to smell more powerful than other dogs reverts back to when dogs were wild creatures running in packs. The pack leader would wish to impress on his subordinates that he was still top dog. Or perhaps a dog lower in the pecking order would attempt to challenge the pack leader, so to give him added courage, he would first roll in strong smelling animal droppings.

Although our pet dogs have been domesticated for centuries, the desire and instinct to cover themselves in, to us, evil smells is still very strong, even though they may not know why they are doing it. It could occur because you are still having a tussle with your dog as to who is boss, so the dog reverts to his instinctive behaviour in an attempt to impress you.

Our reaction to our smelly dogs is firstly to reject them, not wanting them to get near us and secondly, to bath them as soon as possible to get rid of the smell. This can in turn merely heighten the desire for the dog to repeat his rolling actions as soon as he gets the chance.

As with everything that we wish to deter the dog from doing, you can, through corrective training on the lead, show the dog that you do not like this behaviour. The bad news, though, is that in my experience, a determined "roller" will generally remain so.

3

FORMAL TRAINING

Formal training is the process of teaching your dog to perform certain actions in response to certain stimuli. It means putting a collar and lead on the dog and conditioning him to respond instantly to your command.

Types of Collars and Leads

The first step is to select the right collar and lead. I would recommend you use a good quality leather lead, at least three feet long, with a strong trigger type clip for attaching the lead to the collar. Rope and nylon leads do not have the same flexible quality as leather and they can "burn" your hands if pulled through quickly. As to collars, there are many types available:

TRAINING CHAINS. The training chain, or choke chain, is not favoured by most dog trainers and behaviourists. In extreme cases, incorrect fitting and usage can cause damage to the dog's neck. It certainly should NEVER be used on young puppies. Some experienced people do know how to use the chain correctly, but it is not necessary for a pet dog, and other softer collars are now available. However, because they *are* in use, the following information and diagrams are included on selecting a suitable one for your dog, fitting it and how to place it around the dog's neck.

The close-welded link variety is best, as it tends to run more freely through the links at each end. (The open link variety can jam up.) The correct thickness is important – too thin and you will cut the dog's neck, too thick and it

Fig. 2. (Left) Incorrect and (right) correct adjustment for a chain collar.

will be too heavy for the dog. When the chain is around the dog's neck, and adjusted so that it fits snugly (but NOT tightly), there should be about a hand's width of chain left, before it attaches to the lead.

To put the chain on, position the dog next to you by your left leg, both of you facing the same direction. Form the collar into a circle by threading it through one metal ring. With the end that is going to be attached to the lead uppermost, slip the chain over the dog's head. Attach the lead to the free ring and, to check that you have it on correctly, use the lead to GENTLY tighten the collar, then relax the pressure. The collar should slacken instantly. If it doesn't, then the collar is on "upside down".

Finally, I repeat: the use of chain collars is unnecessary. Better and kinder collars are available.

DOUBLE ACTION TRAINING COLLAR. In my experience, this is the best type of training collar, suitable for the majority

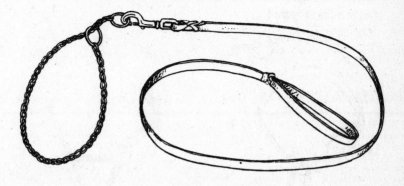

Fig. 3. A chain collar with a suitable leather lead.

of dogs, including puppies. It is made of flat nylon, which is formed into a circle using a connection of a small length of chain, each end of the chain attaching to the nylon via a metal ring, with a third metal ring in the middle of the chain, for attaching the collar to the lead.

These collars are adjustable and come in various sizes, so they are suitable for the smallest of breeds to the largest. Make sure that you get the type with two adjusters on it – you can buy them with only one adjuster, but these tend to slip and consequently need adjusting frequently.

When the collar is fitted around the dog's neck and the lead is attached, pull the lead gently so that pressure is applied to the collar and check that the two metal rings are not meeting. If they are, it means that there will be no "give" in the collar and it will remain tight whether or not you are applying pressure via the lead. Use the adjusters so that when you do tighten the collar, at least half an inch of chain separates the two rings. That way, there is sufficient slack in the collar to relax it once pressure from the lead is stopped.

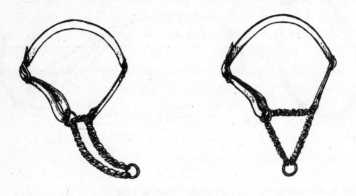

Fig. 4. A double action training collar showing (left) incorrect and (right) correct adjustment.

ROPE AND NYLON SLIP COLLARS. These collars are quite satisfactory once you have achieved control over your dog, but are not recommended to begin your training. They tend not to release very quickly; they keep the pressure on the dog's neck even after you have slackened the lead. This could have an adverse effect and actually hinder the training.

ORDINARY LEATHER COLLARS. You should not try to teach my methods of training using an ordinary collar. These collars only put pressure on the front part of the dog's neck and could end up choking him. Once the dog is controlled and no longer needs collar correction, they are perfectly adequate but until then should only be used as an identification collar, carrying your name and address.

When using a training collar, remove all other collars or they could interfere with the training collar's action.

Remember, whatever type of collar you put onto your dog, to include an identity disc bearing your name and phone number. Legally, your dog *must* carry some form of owner identification. Many people now have their dogs tattooed or microchipped, but, at least to begin with, ensure that he has a disc on his collar. Don't include the dog's name – it makes it easier for thieves to steal him!

How to use the Collar and Lead

Having obtained the right kind of collar and lead and adjusted them correctly, how are you going to use them to train your dog? So far I have only discussed pressure on the dog's neck, but it is most important that you do not rely totally on the lead to control your dog. The collar, via the lead, is used in conjunction with your hands and your voice. Initially, you will be giving the dog verbal and visual signals, *backed up* with a *momentary* pressure on the collar, relaxed the instant the dog complies. Pressure is applied by a "snatch" action, not a pull or tug. If you try to pull on the lead, the dog will simply pull back and you will end up having a tug of war – with him coming out the winner. The neck is used to absorb the pressure, being the strongest part of his anatomy. The sensation the dog feels is uncomfortable but not painful. He learns that by instantly obeying your commands, all pressure is removed, followed immediately by lavish praise and fuss from you.

Although you must not rely on the lead to control your dog there should never be a time when you take him out of the house or garden without being attached to you, via the lead, however well-trained he eventually becomes. Apart from being an offence to have your dog off a lead on a main road, it is stupid and potentially very dangerous to allow him to walk free on *any* road. There is always a chance that he could be startled into doing something unpredictable, or be frightened into dashing into the road. As well as risking his life, he could also endanger the life of other animals, or worse still, other humans.

If, like me, you are a car driver, you may well have experienced the dilemma of seeing a dog walking along off the lead, with the owner several yards away. You have your foot hovering over the brake pedal, wondering if he's about to dash into the road. As the driver of a potentially lethal machine, you may well be put into the position of swerving or braking to avoid the dog, and in the process hit some innocent pedestrian, or at the very least damage someone else's property.

Dog owners are now held responsible for any damage their dogs cause, even indirectly, and it could be a very expensive lesson to learn, both for the owner's pocket and his conscience.

Tones of Voice and Visual Signals

As your voice is one of the most important training aids you are going to use, do remember that your dog does not understand the English language. He hears "sounds" not words, so in theory you can use any word you choose to fit any action, as long as you are consistent. However, it is more realistic for us to use a word that makes sense to us, so we use the word **sit** to get the dog to sit, etc. The tone of the word must be decisive. You don't need to bellow like a sergeant-major, but your voice should convey determination and authority, with you "telling" your dog, rather than "asking" him. Each command must also sound different for each separate action.

After each command you will be rewarding your dog, so use lots of excited, loving sounds, such as "good dog", "super dog", "clever dog" etc., all said in a really happy voice. *Show* him with your hands that you are pleased with him, stroke him lovingly, play with him, let him see that his action of compliance has really pleased you. Praise and reward are *vital* to his learning. Reward every effort, however small.

Some exercises will eventually lead to your controlling your dog when he is some distance away from you, so you will be teaching a visual command as well as a verbal one. If you only train with verbal commands you could, for example, have quite a problem getting your dog back to you when he is 200 yards away and the wind is blowing your voice back in the opposite direction. Or suppose you lose your voice – does that mean you also lose control over your dog? Some dogs become deaf as they grow old. Must that mean he can then do as he pleases, because he can no longer hear you?

By giving him audible and visual signals, he has an even better chance of understanding what you want him to do, so that you are not totally dependent on the lead for control.

Getting the Dog to Pay Attention – Watch
By necessity, this has to be the first lesson. Even if you do everything perfectly, all the signalling and commands will be wasted if the dog is not watching you to begin with. You will be incorporating this exercise into all the others you will be teaching, getting him to "watch" you before giving him any other command.

The aim is to get him to watch you and nothing else, for at least twenty-five seconds at any one time, without moving his head away *at all*. Lack of attention is one of the biggest problems which everyone has when they start training, so it is worth spending time teaching him to watch, before you progress to any of the other exercises. The verbal aids you use are his name, which he should know better than any other sound, and the command

watch me. You can start teaching him when there are no other distractions and on the occasion when your dog has deliberately chosen to come and seek your attention.

At some time, perhaps when you are sitting watching television, your dog comes over to you, nudges your hand with his nose and "asks" you for attention. When this happens, gently guide him around so that he is sitting leaning against your left leg. With your right hand under his chin and your left hand on the top of his head, stroke and tickle his head, into your left leg and upwards so that you have eye contact. At the same time, tell him **good boy**, **watch me**. All the time he is gazing up at you, continue to reward him, repeating the command **watch me**, speaking to him in a soothing voice and telling him how good he is. The second his attention wanders, stop stroking and change your voice to a commanding tone, telling him **watch me** again. Although at this early stage you are not giving him any forcible compulsion to watch, you are building up a very pleasant association with the sound of **watch** and the action of watching. Do this over a couple of days, then you can go on to the next stage.

Having laid the foundations, the next stage is to put him on his collar and lead, and teach him to watch, even when there are distractions going on around him. Sit him by your left leg, with you and he facing the same direction. Hold the lead in your right hand and shorten the lead until your right hand is just a few inches away from his collar. With your hand under his neck, give the collar a little "check", turning his head into your leg and tilt his chin up, so that he is looking directly at you. At the same time, use his name and give the command **watch me**. Your left hand should be placed on the top of his head, stroking and turning his head into your leg at the same time. Keep stroking and verbally rewarding all the time he is watching, until his attention wanders, then stop all stroking and repeat the collar and verbal command.

When he has watched for ten seconds, release him from the exercise and allow him to play. By releasing him, I mean making it clear to the dog that he is off duty and work has finished until you command him again. I teach my dogs a release command, namely **that'll do** and they know that when they hear that sound, they can relax and play. Allow him to play, with you participating, for at least two minutes, then get him back under control and repeat the whole process again. You can, if you wish, also teach him a command that means "back on duty", by saying, "work" or something similar, but if you teach him from the outset that when you tell him **watch me**, he is on duty, that should be sufficient for him to know that he is about to be commanded to perform some action.

Do the whole exercise three or four times for the first day, with two-minute play breaks between each session. On the second day, repeat as before; this time making him watch for fifteen seconds. Continue over three or four days until he will watch for twenty-five seconds without being distracted.

Coming When Called – The Recall

Verbal Command – Dog's name followed by **come**.

Visual Signal – Arms outstretched, either side of your body.

You should have already built the groundwork for this exercise by calling your dog each time you feed him, as suggested in Chapter 2. You will have started to condition the dog to return to you when he hears the sound **come**, by being rewarded for obeying – albeit so far because he wants his dinner!

Now you are going to start teaching him, on the lead, that he must come to you when he hears that sound, even if he doesn't want to. The lead is there to use as an added compulsion if he should ignore the verbal command.

Hold the lead in your right hand and with the dog on your left, walk forward a few paces, letting the dog get in front of you. Then run backwards, calling your dog as you go and stretching your arms out as far as you can, bearing in mind you're holding the lead.

Being attached to the lead he can hardly fail to respond, but if he hesitates even for a fraction of a second after you call him, give him a quick check on the lead, repeating the verbal command. As soon as he starts to respond, praise him verbally and take all pressure off the collar. After running backwards a few paces, stand still and let him catch up with you and then praise him like mad. The visual signal will at this stage obviously be slightly abbreviated, because you are still holding the lead and are at close quarters to your dog, but do give as much of the signal as you can, remembering that later on you will be expecting him to return from a distance. Therefore he must start learning it now. Repeat the exercise two or three times, giving full signals each time and loads of praise when he reaches you. When you have practised the above for two or three days, make the lead longer by attaching a piece of rope or cord to the end, thereby allowing you to get a further distance from your dog before you call him. Let him "wander" around at the end of the lead, enjoying his walk, then stand still and call him, gathering in the excess lead as he comes to you. Remember, full hand, voice and if necessary, lead signals, each time you call him, and *full* praise *every* time he comes back.

Repeat this several times over a few days and when he has complied instantly with your command, you can then let him off the lead. To give you more confidence, choose a nice, safe enclosed area for the first time. If you've taught him properly, he'll come back, so don't worry.

When he comes to your call, praise and praise and praise him, cuddle him, play with him, be really excited. He'll *really* want to come back each time if you make it so enjoyable for him to do so.

There are a few pitfalls still to be avoided. Don't get into the habit of only calling him back when the walk is ended and you are about to return home. If you do, he will very soon come to associate that being called back means the end of his freedom and he will become more and more reluctant to come back to you.

Make a point of calling him to you throughout the walk, always to lots of fuss – that way he won't get to learn *which* call signifies the end of the walk. Likewise, when the walk is ended, don't always call him from the same spot in the park. They quickly learn the route of their walk and if you put him back on his lead at the same spot each time, he will again associate that place with the end of his walk and will soon start to ignore your call.

POSSIBLE PROBLEMS. Your dog may have already learned that once he is off the lead, he can do as he likes and goes very conveniently "deaf". Interesting diversions such as other dogs, people playing football, fascinating smells, etc., are far more compelling than coming back to you when you call. Don't fall into the trap of chasing him, as all this will do is turn the whole thing into a game and your dog is much faster on his feet than you. *Don't*, when he does eventually honour you with his presence, tell him off. Your logic tells you that you are punishing him for keeping you waiting. His "understanding" tells him he is being punished for coming back. Even if you've been trying to get him back for over an hour, reward him like mad when he does come, otherwise next time he'll keep you waiting two hours!

There are things you can do to encourage the reluctant

dog. One: walk away from him pretending indifference. Two: sit on the grass, study something on the ground with great interest. Three: pretend to have something in your hands (you *can* have a tit-bit hidden away in this instance).

Dogs are incredibly curious and he may come back, firstly to check why you're not running after him and secondly, to see what you are finding so interesting. When he does, don't make a grab for him, as he will no doubt manage to evade you. Give him a warm welcome, but continue to be "pre-occupied". Once it's obvious that he's going to settle back with you, calmly take hold of his collar, give him a big fuss, so he will associate pleasure with being restrained, then *let him go again*. If you don't, he will once again connect coming back to you with his fun being curtailed, therefore ensuring that he definitely won't return next time you call. If he is showing interest in someone else and prefers to remain with them rather than come back to you, enlist their help. Ask them to be very unwelcoming towards him. Get them to stamp their feet and shout at him. You, meanwhile, will be ever so welcoming, calling him pleasantly. He will soon decide that it's much better to come back to you rather than stay with those nasty people.

If the problem is really persistent, you may need to go back to basic training. Put him back on a long lead and let it trail on the ground. Once you have decided he is to return to you, you can tread on the trailing lead, to prevent him running away. It's not the ideal answer, but unfortunately there are some dogs who quickly learn that once they're off the lead, there's precious little you can do about it – another good reason for starting the training early.

The following exercise, the **down,** can sometimes help with a persistent "non returning" dog, so study it well, it may be the answer.

Down on Command and Down Stay

Verbal Command – Dog's name and **down**.

Visual Signal – Right arm raised above your head, lowering to floor level.

As with every exercise, you teach your dog, on the lead, to lie down on command, with the eventual aim that he will drop on command from 100 yards away. The **down** is the most submissive action that your dog can make for you. If taught correctly, it will assist you greatly in all aspects of gaining control over your dog.

You may have noticed that when two strange dogs confront one another, one dog will sometimes lay down, often rolling right over onto his back. This action is understood by the other dog as a sign of his own dominance, the underdog having recognised the other as his superior.

Similarly, when two dogs are fighting, the conflict often ends before any damage is done, by one dog giving in to the other by rolling over on his back, acknowledging that the other is stronger and thus pack leader. Therefore, each time you command your dog to lie down and he complies, you are compounding your authority over your dog.

Before you begin teaching him on the lead, you can already have started to condition him to the sound of **down** with the action of lying down, by cheating a little. Every time you see your dog about to lie down naturally, give him the verbal command **down**, telling him "good boy" as he does. By doing this, you're not teaching him to lie down when you say so, but you are teaching him a sound to go with the action.

To teach him to lie down when *you* say so, start with your dog, on the lead, sitting on your left side, against your leg, with you and him both facing the same direction, as shown in fig. 5.

Fig. 5. Ready to start the *down* exercise.

Hold the lead in your right hand and gather up the slack until your right hand is about six inches from the collar. Slide the collar around so that it is under the dog's neck. The lead and hand signal, given together at this stage, is applied by a gentle jerk straight downwards, at the same time you give the verbal command **down**. The action of your right hand will dip the dog's head downwards. As you give the verbal and lead commands, place your left hand, palm downwards, just behind the dog's shoulders and push gently downwards and backwards.

As soon as the dog goes down, take all the pressure off the dog's collar and shoulders and go down to his level and reward him. If he should make any attempt to get up again at this stage, correct him immediately, repeating all signals. Don't worry if he rolls over on his back – as mentioned previously this is a sign of complete submission.

Keep the dog on the floor for about ten seconds, remaining there with him, all the time praising and stroking him. Then release him, using the release command you have taught him during the "watch" exercise, i.e. **That'll do**, and let him get up and play.

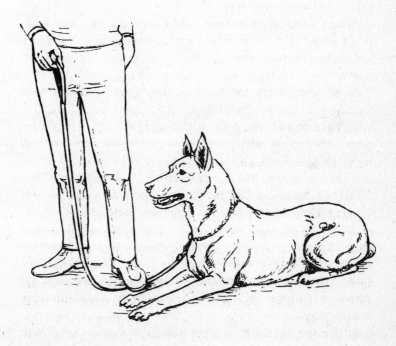

Fig. 6. Place your left foot on the lead . . .

Repeat the exercise three or four times, each time using full signals, staying there with him each time, then releasing and rewarding. The visual signal you are teaching, i.e. the right hand raised and then lowering to the floor, is obviously abbreviated at this stage because of the close proximity to your dog, but you are building up the association of the verbal and visual signal with the required action.

The next stage is to get the dog to remain on the floor whilst you stand up. Command the dog to lie down then carefully place your left foot on the lead, about nine inches from the collar. You should still be holding the end of the lead in your right hand. As you stand up, give him the verbal command **stay**.

When teaching the **stay** command, do not use your dog's name. Use of his name in this context could actually encourage him to move, which is the opposite of what you want.

If he should try to move as you rise, your left foot standing on the lead will apply the pressure to the collar which previously was given with the right hand. Make sure your left foot is not too close to the collar, pinning his head to the floor, just sufficient distance away to allow his head to move, but not enough to allow him to get up. Your left hand can still be used to apply pressure behind his shoulders if he should try to get up rear end first.

Any sign of movement on his part must be corrected immediately, giving full signals – **down . . . stay** – and all the time he remains where he should be, verbally reward him. When he has remained down for ten seconds, go down to his level, praise and release him, again allowing him to play.

It is important that you do not allow him to anticipate his reward by starting to rise as you go down to him. If you let him do this, he will gradually start getting up earlier and earlier, eventually not staying down at all. He must learn to associate that he only gets rewarded whilst he is lying down for this exercise, thus making it unlikely that he will move.

STAYING DOWN AT A DISTANCE. When you have practised for two or three days getting him to stay down whilst you stand up, you can then progress to the next stage – leaving him in the down, whilst you move to the front of him.

Fig. 7. The visual *stay* signal.

This is where you bring in the visual **stay** signal, as well as the verbal command. The signal is given with the left hand, which is placed in front of the dog's face, palm facing towards the dog. You will also start to establish "foot" signals as well. Every time you require your dog to remain in a position while you move away, you will always set off on your right foot first. Your feet are, after all, much nearer to your dog than your face and you will find that if you consistently position your feet in the same pattern when doing a particular exercise, your dog will pick up the additional signal very quickly. So, command the dog to lie down, tell him **stay** and place your left foot on the lead, again about nine inches from the collar, holding the other end of the lead in your right hand. Repeat the verbal command **stay**, plus give the visual command as well. Now start to move your right foot

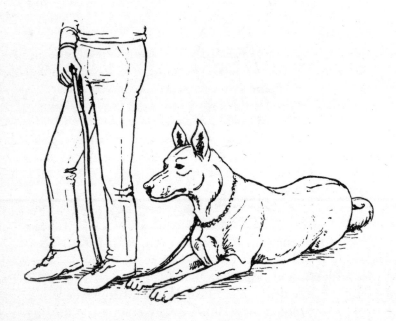

Fig. 8. How you should move away from the *stay* position.

slowly backwards and forwards, in front of his face, keeping the left foot still. This is to get him used to the idea of your moving whilst he remains still, in the down position.

When he has remained still for ten seconds, take a small step with your right foot, turning to face him, so that you are now standing in front of the dog, right up close to his front feet. You will obviously have had to move your left foot as well, but do this very carefully, sliding it around with the lead still underneath.

Take care not to put any pressure on the collar as you move your foot, otherwise your dog may move. Stay in front for about ten seconds, then step back to the side, right foot moving first, stand still next to him for a couple of seconds, then go down to him, reward him lavishly and release him.

Always wait a few seconds after returning back to his side, before going down and releasing him, to prevent him from anticipating the end of the exercise and his reward.

Whenever you move around your dog, move positively. Don't hover, as any sign of uncertainty could be misinterpreted by your dog and could be used as an excuse to move. When he is happily staying down for ten seconds with you standing close in front of him, you can then dispense with keeping the left foot on the lead. Gradually increase the distance, taking one pace at a time, always facing the dog, so that after a few days' practice you can get to the length of the lead away, without the dog moving. Then you can start leaving the lead on the floor, out in front of the dog, without holding the end.

If you have the lead out in front of the dog, where you will be standing, you can quickly take hold of it if the dog should need correcting. Over a period of several days, build up the distance and time, so that after about two weeks you can leave him for a distance of five yards for two minutes. Don't try and be too clever, marching off twenty yards away and leaving him down for ten minutes. One, your dog will quickly get very fed up and two, if he should try to move, you will be too far away to do anything about it. Five yards' distance for two minutes is quite enough for normal purposes.

THE "QUICK" DOWN. To get your dog not only to lie down but to "drop" into the down instantly, is most important for several reasons. Firstly, if at any time during his training he starts to challenge you, you can instantly re-enforce your control. Secondly, however excited he becomes, during play times, you will have a very effective stop switch. Thirdly, and perhaps most importantly, it could be a potential life-saver.

You could get into a situation when, perhaps, you trip and let go of the lead, or the lead breaks, and the dog is frightened and runs into the road. If you can get him to lie down and remain still, he will not be nearly such a hazard to oncoming traffic – a stationary dog being much easier to avoid than one who is running about. Finally, if you have been experiencing trouble getting your dog to come back when called, if you can instil the **down** into him and get him to drop at a distance, you will at least have regained control and be able to go and collect him.

To teach him the quick **down**, put him on his lead and play very excitedly with him for a few seconds, then give him the **down** command, pushing him instantly into the position. Keep him down for a few seconds, then praise and release, then play again. The object is to get him to drop before you can push him down – in other words, for him to avoid the correction by going down before you can push him. Practise this until your dog is literally throwing himself into the position.

Sit and Sit Stay

Verbal Command – Dog's name and **sit**.

Visual Signal – For **sit**, right hand raising up and in front of dog's face.

For **stay**, as you have done in the **down . . . stay**.

Sit is a very basic exercise and one which you have probably already started teaching, with varying degrees of success. You may have found that you can get him to sit, but he springs back up before you want him to. Or he may sit, but not beside you where you want him, either sitting in front of or behind you. So, assuming you have already started building up the association of the word **sit** with the action required, it is probably best if you start back at square one, ensuring that each time, the dog sits immediately and in the position and place you want.

With the dog by your left leg, both of you facing the same direction, hold the lead in your right hand. The length of the lead at this stage depends on the size of your dog and how tall you are. The ideal length is so that, when he is sitting by your side, with you holding the lead in your right hand and with your arm hanging down and resting just above your right thigh, the dog's collar is slack. But the instant you apply pressure by using your right hand on the lead, the collar will tighten.

If you find that you have to lift your right arm right up above your head to put pressure on the collar, then the lead is too long. Using the verbal command **sit**, apply pressure to the dog's collar by raising your right hand up and across your body, in front of the dog's face. The pressure and direction of the signal will lift your dog's head up slightly. At the same time, you will apply gentle pressure, with your left hand, on the dog's rear end, by his left thigh, pushing down and at the same time in towards your leg. *Do not* push on the top of the dog's back as you could well damage his spine. As soon as the dog has sat, take all the pressure off the collar, remove your left hand and reward him. If he should try to move, repeat all commands and signals. Correct him every time he tries to move, making sure you always put him back in the original spot each time. As with every other exercise, he will soon learn that when he remains sitting in the right position he is rewarded, whereas any movement on his part meets with determined correction from you.

Fig. 9. Correct way to position the dog to sit.

SIT . . . STAY. Once he has learned that **sit** means to sit on one spot, the next stage is to teach him to **stay** on that spot while you move away from him. The visual signal for the sit . . . stay is exactly the same as for the down . . . stay. There are, however, three main differences between the sit . . . stay and down . . . stay.

Firstly, do not put your left foot on the lead before starting to move with the right foot. You could well put pressure on the lead via your foot and you have been teaching him that pressure on the collar in a downwards direction means that he is to lie down – the exact opposite of what you are teaching now.

Secondly, before you start moving to the front of the dog, slide the collar around so that the part attaching to the lead is on the TOP of his neck. This is so that when you are in front of your dog, you will easily be able to repeat the lead/hand signal, if he should try to move.

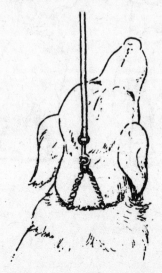

Fig. 10. Correct positioning of collar and lead for the *sit, stay*.

Thirdly, the most important difference is the way you release your dog from the sit . . . stay. When you return back to his side, you are going to make him move *backwards*. You are going to "condition" him that the *only* way he ever moves from this exercise is by going backwards first. Thus it is highly unlikely that he will break the stay, by moving himself backwards then coming

Fig. 11. *Sit, stay,* from the front.

forwards – I've never seen a dog do it yet! It may sound strange, but I assure you it works. So, having told the dog to **stay**, move to the front of him (right foot first), and stay there for ten seconds, as you did for the down . . . stay.

Fig. 12. The *sit-stay* signal from the front without the lead.

Return to the side of your dog, wait a couple of seconds, then physically move the dog backwards, by stepping back yourself, gently guiding the dog back with you, giving him his release command **That'll do**, praise and reward him. Do that *every* time you release him from the sit . . . stay, until you will eventually be able to dispense with any pressure on the collar to move him backwards – he will do it automatically. When you give him the release command, do sound excited, so that he continues to enjoy his training.

As in the down . . . stay, gradually build up the time and distance over a couple of weeks so that he is rock steady at each stage before going on to the next.

Wait

Verbal Command – Dog's name and **wait**.

Visual Signal – One sweep of the left arm, starting from the side of your left leg, over in front of the dog's face – like the pendulum swing of a clock.

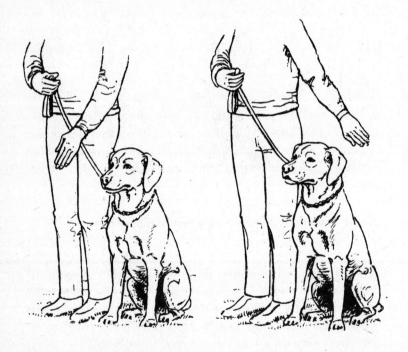

Fig. 13. The hand signal for *wait*.

Having taught your dog that **stay** means "stay where I tell you until I come back to you", you now need to teach

him that **wait** means, "wait where I tell you until I give
you further commands". For example, **wait** whilst the
door is opened before he jumps out of the car; **wait** whilst
the front door is opened properly, rather than trying to
push through it half opened; **wait** while you put his dinner
on the floor, etc.

Some people teach the **stay** to cover all these things,
plus staying in one place, but I firmly believe this confuses
the dog, giving him one command to mean two different
things and expecting him to know which one you mean. It
also encourages him to break the **stay** exercise, as he will
be continually on edge, waiting for further commands. If
you have taught him that **stay** means he *never* moves until
you return to his side, there can be no doubt in his mind
whatsoever. With the **wait**, you are teaching him that he is
to wait until given further instruction.

A word of caution before you start. Please don't
practise the **stay** and **wait** exercises one after the other.
You don't want to give your dog any chance of becoming
confused. Even though the command is different, at the
beginning there is a risk that he may try and anticipate
your wishes.

To begin, start with the dog in the normal position,
beside your left leg. Remember to leave him right foot
first, give him the verbal and visual **wait** commands and
step to the front of him. Remain there for a couple of
seconds, then repeat the verbal command and back away
from him, until you are at the end of the lead (fig. 14).
Stand still and call him to you, rewarding him as he
comes.

If he should move before you call, correct him very
gently by putting him back on the exact spot again. Don't
be too harsh with the correction, as, if you over correct, it
may put him off moving and make him hesitant when you
call him next time. All the time he remains sitting and

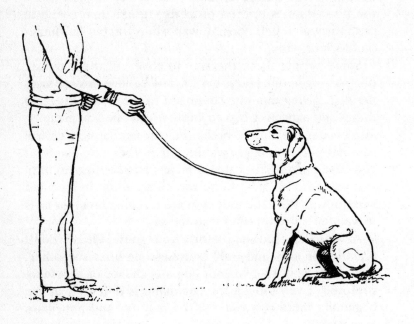

Fig. 14. Dog waiting.

waiting, tell him gently what a good dog he is – don't get too excited at this stage, otherwise again it may encourage him to move before you want him to.

By telling him gently that he is good for waiting, he will understand quicker what he is supposed to be doing. Repeat this two or three times over a couple of days and then start incorporating the **wait** command whenever the situation is appropriate. Getting out of the car is usually

Fig. 15. Hand signal for *come*.

Fig. 16. The dog responds.

where this exercise is most beneficial – there are few things worse, or potentially more dangerous, than a dog which leaps out of the car the instant the door is open. By teaching him the **wait** exercise properly, you will be able to open the car door and know he will not move until you tell him to.

Stand

Verbal Command – Dog's name and **stand**.

I'm sure that some readers are wondering why on earth they should teach their dog to stand on command and what practical purpose it would serve. Well, how about when you brush your dog? What about when he comes back from a muddy walk and you have to dry him? Think about when you have to take the dog to the vet – it's much easier for the vet to examine him if he's standing nice and still. I'm sure you can think of other occasions within your own lives when it would be very convenient if he stood still on command.

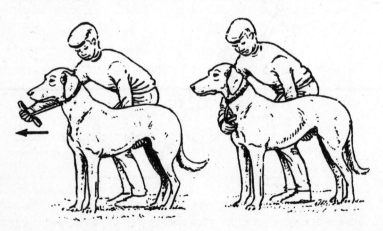

Fig. 17 The "stand".

The **stand** is the gentlest of all exercises to teach and also one of the easiest. The verbal command **stand** is given very gently, unlike all other commands you have been using and is delivered in a "sing-song" type of voice. It must sound completely different from the authoritative commands of **sit** and **down**. The aim is to teach him that on receiving the verbal and visual commands, he will stand up, keeping his front feet still and moving his back feet *backwards*.

Start as always with the dog on your left, in the sit position. Slide the collar under his neck and gather up the lead in your right hand, until your hand is just a couple of inches from his collar. The direction you signal the collar is directly out in front, gently pulling his head forward, but not making him walk forward. Your voice says **stand** at the same time.

The dog will not yet understand what he is supposed to do, so you are going to assist him into the position with your left hand. Place your hand between the dog and your left leg. Put your hand under his tummy and gently lift him up and backwards, tickling his tummy as you lift. As soon as he is up, take all the pressure off the collar, but leave your right hand on his chest, to prevent him moving forwards and leave your left hand tickling his tummy. He will no doubt remain in that position very willingly, as he is receiving such lovely inducement to do so. Eventually you will want him to stand solely on the verbal command, so don't make the mistake of relying on the lead and your hands to make him stand – give him the **stand** sound each time you assist him into the position.

You might think that it would be much easier for you to place your left arm *over* the dog to lift and tickle, rather than placing it between you and the dog. What you will find, if you do that, is that your dog will tend to lean towards the arm that is tickling, with the result that he will be leaning away from you, rather than leaning towards you, which is what you want.

You may also find that once he stands, he starts to walk forward. This is because you are putting too much pressure on the collar as you pull forwards, plus you are not putting your hand on his chest quickly enough. Perhaps, too, you have your lead too long to begin with.

You may also find that as soon as you have positioned the dog into the stand, he immediately goes to sit again. You could be causing this, by pulling up on the lead, which, as the dog has already learned, means **sit**. Do be careful, therefore, not to put any upward pressure on the collar once he has stood.

Finally, you may find this exercise easier to begin with if you kneel down to the dog's level to give the signal – especially if you have a small dog.

Walking to Heel

Verbal Command – Dog's name and **heel** or **close** (choose one and stick to it).

I suspect that some readers may have jumped straight to this section, as it is probably the one thing that causes more problems than any other. However, if you have skipped the previous pages, it would be in your own interest to go back and read them first. Everything taught so far has been designed to get overall control of your dog, culminating in making this exercise easier to teach.

You will be teaching your dog to walk on his lead, by your left leg, with his shoulder level with your knee and without pulling or jumping up. You will be using your voice, hands and lead to show him where he should be. As with all exercises, your voice and hands will be the prime form of correction and reward. Don't rely on the collar, via the lead, to keep the dog in the correct place.

Start with your dog sitting, against your left leg. Hold the lead in your right hand and hang your right arm down naturally, so that it is resting on the front of your right thigh. The lead should be just long enough so that with the dog sitting beside you, there is no pressure on the collar, but should he move from the sit position, the collar will tighten. This is shown in fig. 18. Don't have the lead so short that the collar is permanently tight.

Fig. 18. Prior to starting *heel* work.

You will be using the lead to give a directional signal, via the collar, across your body to your right hand. With young puppies you should keep any collar correction to an absolute minimum, as their necks are still growing. Use your voice and hands as the main stimuli.

Decide which verbal command you are going to use and stick to it. If you decide upon **heel**, try to pronounce it "heyall", otherwise, it tends to sound rather flat. If you decide to use **close**, pronounce it as "clowss".

You will be stepping off with your *left* foot first, as in this exercise you want him to accompany you. (In the **stay** and the **wait**, you stepped off right foot first, as he was to remain behind.) Give him full commands – his name, **watch me** and the heel command, signalling the collar with a quick snatch and step off, taking one pace only, then stopping and telling the dog **sit** as you stop.

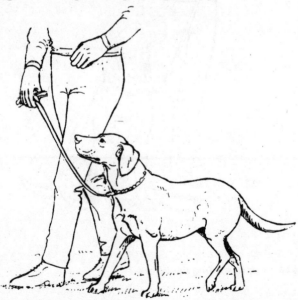

Fig. 19 Dog walking by handler's left leg.

Taking one pace only will not have given him much chance to pull, but it will give you the opportunity to show him what all the signals mean. There is no point galloping off for several yards at this stage. So, for the first lesson, it will be one pace at a time. Reward the dog every chance you get. By rewarding, I mean that every second or fraction of a second that he is walking with you and not pulling, take all the pressure off the collar and tell him that he's doing what you want. Use your left hand to fuss him under the chin when he's walking nicely.

Fig. 20. Dog walking nicely, gets reward.

Practise the whole exercise, one pace at a time, for no more than two minutes, then release the dog, take his lead off and have a good romp with him. After a couple of minutes' play, put him back on the lead, set him up again in the sit position by your left leg and repeat the whole process for a further two minutes, after which more playtime. This is quite enough for the first lesson. Leave the training for at least a couple of hours then put him back on his lead, ready for the next stage. This time you will be taking two paces at a time for a further two minutes, again another play break of two minutes, then another two minutes' training. You will have then done enough for the first day.

Always let him have a good romp between each session – don't try and short-cut the process by leaving it out. You want him to enjoy learning and walking on the lead. Far

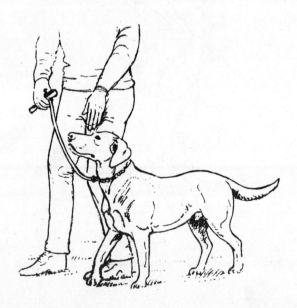

Fig. 21. Walking to *heel,* lead at correct length.

too many dogs are seen being dragged along the road, tails down, faces miserable, so don't let your dog become like that. Make the training fun.

The next day, start off by taking two paces at a time, then slowly progress until you are walking about ten paces before stopping. Correct him every time he pulls, with a rapid snatch on his collar, reward him every time he is in the right place and all the time he remains there. Use your left hand to encourage him, patting the front of your left leg, not the side, or you will find he will hang back to be near your hand. Again, with your left hand, stroke his head and body, gently pull and tickle his ears, fuss him

Fig. 22. Walking to *heel*, lead too long.

under his chin, etc. All pleasant and enjoyable things to encourage him to be with you, rather than pulling.

When he is walking nicely, tell him what a clever, good dog he is at every opportunity. Again, train for only two minutes at a time, then release him and let him have his playtime.

PROBLEMS SO FAR. You may have found that as soon as you stepped off, the dog was out in front, at the end of the lead, before you could signal him via the collar. This is probably because you have the lead too long, as in fig. 22, and therefore cannot get the signal through to the collar in time. Remember what you are trying to teach your dog.

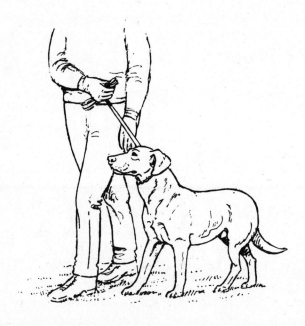

Fig. 23. Walking to *heel*, lead too short.

Every time he tries to pull, the correction must be instant and repetitive. Every attempt he makes to walk without pulling, however slight, must be rewarded with a slack collar and lots of reward.

You may actually be causing the dog to pull, by having the lead too short and the collar too tight. Any attempt to hang on to him via the lead will result in him fighting you and the restriction, as shown in fig. 23. When it comes to pulling power, your dog will win every time – by holding him back, you cause him to set his neck and you cannot give the rapid *tighten then slacken* signal on an already tight lead.

If he tries to pull hard, off-balance him by taking a sideways step, to the right, signalling the collar at the

Fig. 24. Lead held incorrectly, left hand positioned half way up.

same time. Work hard on the **watch** exercise too. If he is paying attention to you, he will not be getting out of position, because the act of watching will put his head in the correct place, by your left leg.

You may be holding the lead with your left hand as well as your right, perhaps with the left hand half way up the lead, as shown in fig. 24, attempting to stop the dog getting in front of you. This ties up your left hand, when you should be using it to reward and encourage the dog and also when you want him to sit. It is a counter-productive action. When you apply the signal with your right hand, the first object that the signal connects with is your left hand and not, as you want, the dog's collar.

Perhaps you are trying to hold the lead just in your left hand. Again, you need that hand for positioning the dog, plus you will find that you cannot give the lead signal in the correct direction – across your body to your right – but instead you are pulling the lead back, behind the dog.

You could be walking at the wrong pace for your dog, therefore not allowing him to get into his natural stride and making him walk unevenly. If you walk too fast, you either end up leaving him behind, or he tries to race you. Too slow and you give him more chance to be distracted. Try to get a happy medium and both of you will find it easier.

Perhaps you have the opposite problem from pulling – the dog is lagging behind you and hanging in his collar. Although you still need to correct such action, use lots of encouragement to get him walking in the correct place, both verbally and with your hands.

It may be necessary to take all pressure off the collar. Turn and face him, run backwards and call him. As soon as he is willingly walking towards you, turn around and walk alongside him, talking to him in an excited voice.

The odd tit-bit can be used as an occasional added inducement. Basically, he needs to find his feet, so keep the pressure off the collar, tell him he's doing it right and soon he'll be walking properly.

Don't bore the dog by endlessly marching about. A few minutes' practice every day is quite enough, making sure the training is happy and interesting and rewarding at every opportunity. Change direction frequently, especially if the dog isn't paying attention. A change of direction, done smartly, will give you a good opportunity to signal your dog and, even better, a chance to reward him afterwards for responding to your commands.

Try practising heelwork on the spot, without moving forwards. With the dog sitting beside you, give him full signals and do a quarter turn to your right. Repeat several times, commanding the dog each time and positioning him in the **sit** after each turn. Turn about on the spot, turning away from the dog again with full signals. All this will help get the message through to the dog. When he receives the heel commands, he must always move with your left leg.

GETTING THE DOG TO RETURN TO HEEL FROM ANY POSITION.

There will be times when your dog manages to position himself in the wrong place, just as you want to start walking with him. You have probably been "scooping" him back to your left side with your hands, which will only have made him want to sit incorrectly even more. He likes being touched and so repeats the action which makes you touch him!

Using the commands which, by now, will be meaning **heel** to the dog, you are going to show him how to get there on his own, without your having to touch him. Obviously you will use exactly the same signals as you have been using to teach him to be by your left leg, as this is where you want him to be.

To show him how to move into the correct position, he must first of all be in the wrong one. For the purpose of teaching, start with him sitting in front of you – something which happens very easily if you are too slow with the **sit** command when you come to a halt.

To set this up, incorporate the **wait** command which you

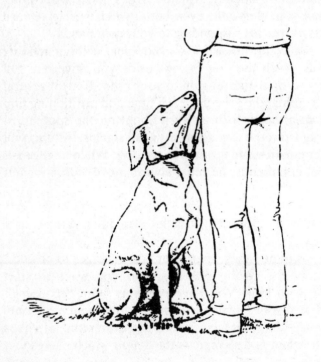

Fig. 25. Ready to return to the *heel* position.

have already taught him. Start with him sitting by your left leg, command him to **wait** and step around to face him, close to his front feet, as in fig. 25. Now you are going to stand still and he is going to move around behind you, going past your right leg and ending up on your left-hand side.

Gather the lead up in your right hand, give him the verbal **heel** command and, at the same time, apply a little

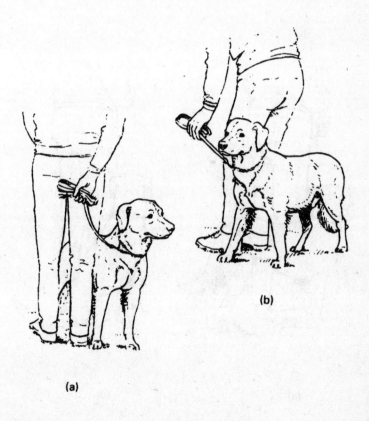

(b)

(a)

Fig. 26. Being guided round behind the handler.

pressure to the collar by giving it a little tug. This is to get him up and moving towards your right leg. See fig. 26(a). As soon as his head is level with your right leg, you must change the lead over into your left hand. Reach your left arm around behind you and take the lead from your right hand, at the same time giving the lead another gentle tug, accompanied with another verbal **heel** command. Guide

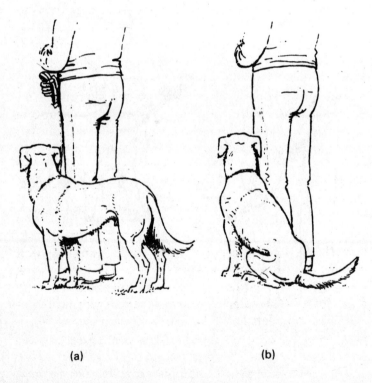

(a)   (b)

Fig. 27. Coming to the right position; completing the exercise.

the dog around behind you (fig. 26(b)), until his head becomes level with your left leg, change the lead back into your right hand, completing the dog's positioning at the same time (fig. 27(a)), and telling him to **sit** (fig. 27(b)).

Now, all that is a great deal more complicated to write down than actually do! Follow the pictures carefully and you will see it is quite simple really. It helps if your dog can see your face as he is coming around behind you. Once he is up and moving, turn your head around to your left, so that you can see him coming and greet him as he comes around. Remember to keep your feet still. You must remain stationary; he is moving to you, not you to him.

If you are having trouble getting the initial movement from your dog (i.e. getting him up from the sit position), you can, just to start with, take a step back with your right foot as you give him the first heel signal on the collar. This gives you a little more "impetus". As soon as he is up and moving, you must put your right foot level with the left one. Don't leave it out behind you, or your dog will have to walk out and around you to get to the heel position, making him go very wide and giving you more trouble in controlling him.

When you've practised this exercise a few times and your dog understands what you want, start getting him to come to heel from any direction. Again using the **wait** command, start with him sitting by your left leg, tell him **wait** and step forward one pace, stand still and call him up to heel, using full commands and signals. Again, with him sitting by your left leg, take a step sideways, away from him, then call him to heel, this time continuing to walk forwards as he comes to you.

If you are determined and patient, it will not be long before your dog is walking beautifully on the lead. Be consistent, be very pleasant and loving when he does it right and he will soon "give in" and actually enjoy his confinement on the lead.

4

THE AGGRESSIVE DOG

Sadly, some dogs are, or become, aggressive. It is difficult to generalise over possible cures without seeing and assessing each individual case, but I will go into some of the causes and suggest ways to cope.

If you have a dog who likes to bite, be it other dogs, strangers, family members or even yourself, you may possibly have already thought about muzzling him, re-homing him, or even having him put to sleep.

A muzzle, or some other kind of head restraint, may well stop him from biting, but it won't teach him *not* to, nor help you to find out why he wants to bite in the first place. Re-homing him is simply passing on the problem to somebody else, which is hardly very fair to them or to the dog. The last resort, having the dog painlessly destroyed, should only be considered when you have explored every possible avenue available to you.

What makes a dog aggressive? It could be anything from bad treatment in a previous home, accidental mistreatment, or poor basic training, through to poor breeding or medical ailments.

Bad Treatment in a Previous Home
If you have a "rescued" dog, you may well not have been given the real reason why the dog needed a new home, either by a previous owner or the rescue kennels,

even if they knew the true reason in the first place.

People who mistreat dogs fall into two groups – those who are deliberately cruel or those who are cruel through ignorance. The result however is the same, a dog who is confused, who will use aggression either to protect himself, or to get his own way.

Despite the bad treatment and subsequent confusion, the dog will still feel insecure when he leaves his "family" and enters a new one. At first he may behave gratefully and, depending on the basic nature of the dog, this period may be very short, or last for ages. Provided that you are consistent in what you will allow him to do and what you will not permit, in a fair and logical way, the dog should settle in with his new family and will know where he stands. However, if his treatment in the previous home was not consistent, or indeed was deliberately cruel, at some stage he will try to test you, in an attempt to establish his position within the new pack.

If, in the past, he has used aggression as a form of self defence against unfair treatment, or to get what he wanted, he may try to continue to use that behaviour with you. Your reaction to any show of aggression from your dog should depend on the circumstances which initially provoked it.

It may be that the dog has learned to steal and guard a "trophy", hiding under a table or chair. Here you should avoid a confrontational approach. DO NOT be tempted to drag him out – there lies the path to being bitten! Leave the dog alone, vacate the room, shutting the door behind you. Leave him for half an hour, then return, acting calmly and avoiding eye contact with him. He'll probably come to greet you, leaving his "den" and his trophy. IGNORE the stolen item, make a fuss of the dog and leave the room again, this time letting him follow you – don't call him out, or he'll probably rush back to get the item. Give him a treat, and making sure he doesn't follow you, go back into the room and remove the offending item!

In future, try to prevent that situation happening. If he's stealing things and bolting to a place of safety, then ensure that there is nothing around to steal! If he's just using the "bolt-holes" to avoid you, or avoid what he thinks is going to be punishment, remove access to these areas – block them up, move furniture, etc.

In milder cases, when the dog may just "grumble" at you, say, for instance, he doesn't want to be brushed, or dried with a towel, a firm NO and a steady stare at the dog should be enough. He may well have been hurt in the past when being groomed, so it is hardly surprising that he should defend himself. Don't shout or scream at him – that will just make him grumble even more. Assuming he does stop, this is one case when you DON'T tell him he's a good dog – you only reward the dog when he does something good, not for NOT doing something naughty! When the grumbling stops, just speak calmly to the dog, then make him do something, i.e. sit or down, which you can then reward. This will also further support your role as pack leader – insisting that the dog perform some task for you, which you can then praise.

Once you have established the "trigger" which provokes the dog, you can either ensure that these situations are avoided, or set up a controlled situation, in order to overcome them. It may be a particular noise, person, place or thing which triggers the defensive aggression.

As an example, let's use the case of a dog whose previous owner used to beat him. Suppose the owner also had a motor-bike and consequently wore a crash helmet. The dog therefore has a remembered association between people wearing crash helmets and pain. You may have owned the dog for some time, but during that time the dog has not come into contact with anyone wearing a helmet. Then one day an innocent visitor arrives at your house by motor-bike and enters your home, either wearing or carrying the helmet. Suddenly, your previously placid, friendly dog becomes a snarling, biting maniac. Exit one visitor, hopefully not hurt, but definitely unimpressed! Your next step is to borrow a crash helmet. Start to treat it as an extension of yourself, carrying it around with you, leaving it beside your chair when you sit down. Be very calm and casual about it, not making any direct reference to the helmet as far as the dog is concerned. Of course, any aggressive displays must be corrected in the way previously described. Once the dog is used to you walking around with the helmet, start wearing it for a few minutes, several times a day. When he accepts that, leave the helmet by the dog's bowl, until he accepts it completely and ignores it.

The next stage is to set up a dummy situation, of a visitor wearing the helmet and arriving at your house. Enlist the help of a member of the family, or a friend whom the dog knows and likes. Make sure the visitor has plenty of dog-type tit-bits in his pocket. Invite the visitor in, sit him down and talk calmly to him and the dog. Provided there has been no sign of aggression from the dog, the visitor is to offer the dog a tit-bit, talking to him very calmly and quietly. He must not make any sudden moves, or try to touch the dog at this stage.

The slightest hint of aggression must be dealt with by you, not the visitor. When all has been calm for about ten minutes, the visitor can start to stroke the dog, again offering more tit-bits.

Once the dog is totally at ease with the visitor, tell him to remove the helmet and place it on the floor beside him. Try putting a tit-bit inside the helmet, encouraging the dog to seek it out. Repeat this whole procedure two or three times over a couple of weeks, using different people each time.

What you are showing the dog is that the situation, i.e. a person wearing a helmet, is no longer a threatening one for him and nothing dreadful is going to happen, so long as he behaves himself. If he does misbehave, you are going to correct him. All the time he is good, he receives affection and reward, in the shape of stroking and tit-bits.

Eventually, people wearing crash helmets will only provoke pleasant associations for the dog – you may even end up with him actively seeking out people wearing helmets. However, that's another problem!

Apply this type of therapy to whatever is provoking the dog into defensive aggressive behaviour. Remember, correct all shows of aggression, reward all acts of compliance.

Accidental Mistreatment

This could range from you accidentally treading on your dog's foot, to touching the dog where he has an injury of which you were unaware. Such occasions will stick in your dog's mind as an experience which he will not want repeated.

Let's assume that you have accidentally stepped on your dog and he flies out at you, perhaps even biting you in the process. You may well be inclined to forgive him because it was your fault. However, he will remember that not only did it hurt him when you trod on him, but that you allowed the aggressive retaliation which followed. After that, any time anyone steps near his feet, he will repeat the behaviour which you accepted and he will try to bite.

So, as previously described with the helmet situation, he must learn that aggressive behaviour will not be accepted and that, because you once trod on his foot and caused him pain, the same thing is not going to happen every time someone steps near him.

Put the training collar on the dog and attach the lead.

Command him to lie down by your side. Get a member of the family to approach the dog gradually, one step at a time. Any grumbling or snapping must be corrected instantly. All the time he lies there quietly, speak to him in a soothing tone, occasionally stroking him. Don't allow him to back away from the feet, as that way he will not only be avoiding them, but also your correction. Take plenty of time over this stage – if necessary do it over several days, five minutes twice a day, say, for a week.

Once the dog is happy with the feet approaching him slowly and eventually standing still beside him, get the person to move slowly around the dog. They can now start to give the odd tit-bit as an added reward for his good behaviour. Assuming your helper is wearing soft shoes or slippers, have them start gently stroking the dog with their feet. Progress from this to placing a tit-bit on his foot. This will not encourage the dog to eat feet! The opposite will happen, feet will become pleasant objects, not painful ones.

When you have achieved all this, change places with your helper and repeat the whole process, this time getting the dog used to *your* feet being close to him and touching him. Start walking more quickly towards him. Don't forget to reward the dog verbally all the time he shows no sign of aggression. You don't want him to get into the habit of only tolerating feet near to him if food is offered. Get every member of the family to go through this procedure, as well as any friendly visitors, so that eventually feet will no longer hold any fear for him.

Incorrect Basic Training

Dogs do not naturally know right from wrong. Unfortunately many owners unintentionally allow their dogs to become aggressive, by permitting certain behaviour. This is especially so with young puppies, when signs of aggression are allowed because "he's only a baby". It can also happen when you give a home to a rescued dog. You try to compensate him for the trauma he has gone through, by being too soft and feeling sorry for him.

In the same way, dogs who are not given the opportunity to socialise with other people and/or dogs, will often show aggressive tendencies when they do eventually come into contact with people and dogs they do not know.

It is obviously better for all concerned to socialise the dog properly. By socialise, I mean regular interaction with other people, dogs, other animals, places, etc. During this socialising time you can teach the dog, using the corrective methods previously described, the type of behaviour you expect and the behaviour which you will not tolerate.

Introduce the dog properly to the world outside his home. Then he will not feel threatened by other people or dogs. There is often a tendency for under-socialised dogs to be protective towards their owners. Most dogs, once they are secure with those they know well, will assume that strangers are equally trustworthy, unless those strangers show warning signs to the contrary.

Some people, either deliberately or through ignorance, may tease the dog into aggressive behaviour. Children, especially those who have not been taught to respect animals, often end up the victim of their own actions, when a dog retaliates against constant teasing.

Other people may be genuinely afraid of dogs, giving off confusing "vibes" to the dog, which could cause him to act in an aggressively defensive manner.

You are responsible to and for your dog, so you must correct any aggression he shows, be it to humans or animals. Depending on the circumstance, whether or not the dog is reacting to deliberate provocation, you must show him that such behaviour will not be tolerated. If the provocation is deliberate, you can of course take the provoker to task. If the subject of the dog's aggression has innocently sparked off the situation, try to explain, in a reasonable manner, what the action was which initiated the dog's behaviour.

When you have corrected the dog, command him to lie down, or sit, at your feet, so that you can finish the incident by rewarding the dog for obeying your instruction. Assuming that the dog is on a lead at the time, do make sure that once he has complied with your wishes, all pressure via the lead is taken off the collar. A tight lead can indicate to the dog that there is something to be on guard against. In the same way, tightening the lead in an attempt to stop him showing aggression in the first place will probably provoke him further, into an aggressive display. It can also make the dog feel safe, as by hanging on to him, you are effectively keeping him out of trouble. The dog then feels that you are protecting him, which encourages aggressive displays, as you are not going to let him get hurt.

With the dog either sitting or lying down at your side, with the lead slack, the dog recognises that you are in control and that there is no need for him to act defensively.

If you have been guilty of continually keeping your dog out of trouble when he exhibits aggressive behaviour, this could lead to him resenting others coming close to you, as you are his protector. The intervention of another person can threaten his security, which results in his being over-protective. He will resent anyone attempting to sit next to you and either through aggression, or persistent attention-seeking behaviour, will try to undermine the other person, until they remove themselves.

Human nature being what it is, displays like this are often misinterpreted as the dog seemingly being devoted to you, which is very good for your ego. Because it appears that the dog wants you all to himself, you are inclined to tolerate the behaviour and, worse, condone it by getting the other person to move away. It is up to you to show the dog that, much as you love him, you will not tolerate such intervention between you and another person.

Sometimes, the dog is allowed to develop possessive feelings towards food, toys, furniture or territory.

It is a popular misconception that it is natural for a dog to growl at anyone who ventures near whilst he is eating his food or chewing on a bone. If the dog is permitted to get away with intimidating behaviour over something as important to him as food, he will almost certainly use aggression to achieve lesser goals.

The method described at the beginning of the book when feeding puppies can be used just as effectively with an adult dog, and you must persist until the dog realises he only gets these things because you let him.

The more confident your approach when taking food or bones from him, the quicker he will respond in an acceptable fashion. Quick, firm correction, using the dog's collar or, if he isn't wearing one, his scruff, followed by praise when he submits, will re-enforce your position of pack leader.

The same method should be used if the dog shows possessive traits with his toys. He must be taught that he owns nothing and only has access to toys, etc., if you say so.

It is most important that you and other members of the family are consistent with permission and denials. For instance, if you do not want the dog to play with slippers, but another member of the family gives him a slipper to play with, this will confuse the dog over what is and is not acceptable behaviour. It will also undermine your authority with the dog, making future confrontations harder to deal with.

This also applies to territory and furniture. Either the dog is allowed on the settee or he is not. Either he is allowed in the bedrooms, or he is not. He must not be allowed by some members of the family, yet corrected for being there by others. He will become very confused by this and a confused dog is potentially an aggressive dog. You *can* train him, for example, that he is only allowed on the furniture when he is invited, but first he has to learn that he is only there because you say he can be.

Don't make the mistake of thinking that if others allow him to have, or do, things which you don't, that he will love them more and you less. A dog is much more secure when he knows exactly where his place is and is also much more secure when he can instantly recognise who is the leader of his "pack".

Mouthing and Play-Biting

Last in this category of poor basic training comes the dog who likes to mouth your hand and sometimes other parts of your body and your clothes. If you have a puppy you may well be experiencing this, but those of you with adult dogs may also be having trouble with this, caused through illogical training when the dog was a youngster.

You may have already tried shouting at the dog, or slapping his nose, but these actions can actually make the problem worse, and could indeed actively encourage the dog to attempt to bite, initially in play but eventually getting more serious.

To use the logical approach, remember back to when your dog was in the litter, with his brothers and sisters. By play-fighting, one of the lessons the puppy learns is **bite-inhibition**. When one puppy bites another puppy too hard, the bitten puppy yelps or squeals loudly, sometimes snapping back or sometimes running away. Either way, the game is usually called to a halt, and the "biter" learns that his actions caused the game to end. Likewise, if **he** gets bitten too hard during the game, he will squeal etc., to let the other puppy know that he is being too rough. The puppies learn, by their littermates' reactions, to modify their biting and to treat each other more gently.

What we as owners should now do is use the same reaction when the puppy or dog goes to place its teeth on you. Scream loudly "OUCH", or better still, try to yelp like a puppy would. The more dramatic your reaction, the more effect it will have on the dog. Pretend to sulk for a few seconds, in an "I'm not playing with you if you're going to be so rough" attitude. Then offer your hand back to the dog, saying softly "gently" – and if the dog nudges or licks your hand, tell him what a clever dog he is. You may need to repeat this a few times, but the dog will learn, as he did with his brothers and sisters, that biting is a no-no.

Do not encourage rough or competitive play with your dog at any time, especially with children. When their play gets too boisterous, this is when the dog can get over-excited and will start to mouth again. It is not that the dog is automatically aggressive – to him it is natural to use his teeth, but unfortunately this can lead to the dog hurting you and in turn ends up with you losing your temper, shouting at the dog and perhaps slapping him, in an attempt to re-gain control. Although seemingly logical to us, the louder and more physical you become, the more the dog gets "wound up", resulting in him attempting to bite harder, possibly ending up doing serious damage.

Chase type games should always be avoided, as this encourages the dog to jump and bite, either at clothes or hands. Similarly, games with tug type toys should also be avoided. These types of game place the dog in a competitive situation – if he wins the "trophy" it will re-enforce his opinion that he is top dog and will hinder future training. If you win, through brute force, it will make the dog even more determined to use his stronger qualities, i.e. his teeth, in any future confrontation over perceived trophies.

It is instinctive for a dog to try to win in a confrontation – that is how he survived in the wild. What we have to do is to make the "losing" as pleasant and as non-confrontational as possible. When he tries to chew you or your clothes, give him something he *can* chew, such as a toy. As previously mentioned, try not to get involved in situations where one of you has to physically win. For example, don't be tempted into chasing after the dog if he steals something, as this again will become a win or lose situation. (See also *Dogs who Steal*, page 31.) Encourage him to give up what he has stolen by offering an alternative that he *is* allowed, or better still, in this case offer him food as a reward – food is, after all, his number one priority.

Remember that for a dog to use his teeth to "hold" things, be it us or our clothes, is all quite natural for the dog and is not wrong – it is simply that it is not acceptable to us and we have to make it clear to the dog that we will neither encourage such behaviour nor allow it to develop.

Being Bitten by Another Dog

If your dog has been intimidated, attacked or bitten by another dog, he may make a point of avoiding that particular dog, dogs of that particular breed, or indeed all dogs. However, it can affect him the other way – he might actively want to attack that dog, breed type or all dogs.

Both these reactions are understandable and naturally

you will have great sympathy with the dog's feelings. In the first instance, if you allow him to avoid the dog and over-protect him, you could actually make him more nervous. Of course, if the attacker is a known aggressive dog, not being properly controlled by the owner, it is common sense for you to avoid it and take whatever action you deem appropriate to prevent the situation happening again.

If it was just a one-off incident, over-protection by you will lead to him being even more wary. Seek assistance from a dog training club, where they will help you to regain the dog's confidence.

For the dog who begins to respond in an aggressive fashion to *all* other dogs, you must correct him quickly. To the dog, he sees his actions as getting in first, before the other dog can attack him. This will end up with him trying to attack innocent dogs and before long he will become known as "that aggressive dog whose owner can't control him". Your walks with the dog will turn into a nightmare, with people keeping their dogs away from yours and you having to keep the dog on a lead all the time. Proper socialising, with appropriate correction and reward, should sort this out.

Leaving his Natural Mother at the Wrong Age

Sometimes, either through ignorance on the part of the breeder, or circumstances such as the bitch dying, puppies are taken from their natural mother too early. The ideal age for a pup to leave his mum is between seven to nine weeks, which is the crucial man-bonding time. Leaving mum and his litter brothers and sisters before this time means that he misses out on vital parts of his formative education and development.

The bitch teaches her pups what behaviour is acceptable, by admonishing them very firmly when they step out of line. She shows them, by example, how to interact with humans, what to be wary of and what things and situations are harmless.

Leaving his litter brothers and sisters too soon, he will not have completed learning the rules of behaviour when encountering other dogs. By play fighting in the litter, he learns how to moderate his behaviour so as not to cause discomfort, by experiencing early on what over-boisterous behaviour provokes in his litter mates. He learns the correct postures and signals to use when encountering another dog. If this learning is curtailed by leaving the litter before seven weeks old, he will not recognise these signals when he meets his first strange dog and may react in an aggressive fashion. Likewise, because *he* will be giving out confusing signals to the strange dog, that dog may act aggressively, because he is confused by the behaviour he is encountering.

This particularly applies when pups are orphaned at birth and hand-reared by humans. They tend to form a very deep attachment to the person who rears them, which in turn can lead to the pup being very possessive towards people. Not having had the benefit of another canine's teaching in proper dog behaviour, they are inclined to feel antagonistic towards other dogs, as they feel themselves to be human rather than canine.

The reverse can happen if the pup stays with his mum too long, i.e. beyond nine weeks. Because he remains in a dog-oriented environment beyond the man-bonding time, he will relate more easily with dogs than with people, resulting in him being uneasy in human company, which could show itself as either very nervous behaviour or in displays of aggression.

If any of the above applies to your dog, you must pay great attention to socialising him, being scrupulously clear with your correction and reward. It would be very helpful if you could befriend someone who has a docile female dog, as she can help with showing your dog, in canine language, what behaviour is acceptable. Joining a dog training club could well help with finding a suitable companion for this purpose.

You may never achieve complete success in your attempts to mix your dog with other dogs and people, but you should achieve a level at which your dog can co-exist with both.

Poor Breeding

Although the majority of breeders are very selective, there are unfortunately many people who breed from unsuitable stock, often for very dubious reasons.

Some people breed from their bitch in the mistaken belief that it will "be good for her to have a litter". Even worse are those who breed from a bitch who has a poor temperament because they think it will improve it. Others breed simply with an eye to making money from the sale of the litter and, worst of all, are the puppy farmers, who over-breed their bitches, without giving a thought either to temperament, or to the health of the bitch or her pups.

Some of these people may well check the bitch and prospective stud dog for genetic faults, but do not give the same attention to the temperament of the prospective parents. Their offspring will inherit character traits from them both. Often the bitch is bred from far too early, without being given the chance to mature properly, either mentally or physically. As already mentioned, a bitch teaches her pups much by example and if she is nervous or immature, she will pass her own fears and phobias on to her offspring.

Inexperienced or ignorant breeders often fail to give correct advice to new owners, particularly when the owners find the dog showing character traits which they cannot understand, and ask for help. If poor breeding could be the reason why your dog is showing aggressive signs, you will need patience, positive training and the help of a good dog training club, to help you get the best from your dog.

Choosing a Breeder

Whilst on the subject of breeding, if you are reading this book prior to getting your puppy, do make sure that you choose the breeder very carefully. Don't be tempted to buy the puppy which gazes at you appealingly from the nearest pet shop window. Although there are good pet shops, there are also plenty who do not enquire too deeply into the origins of their stock. It is also advisable to avoid the one-off private breeder, who may fall into one of the categories previously mentioned, or at best will not have the expertise needed to raise a litter properly.

The safest way to obtain a puppy is either by personal recommendation, or, once you have decided on the particular breed you want, obtain a list of registered breeders from the Kennel Club.

Before you go and see the puppies, find out about any genetic defects which can occur in your chosen breed. Ask the breeder if both the bitch and the stud dog have been tested for these defects. For some conditions, such as hip dysplasia, there are schemes for submitting the results of such tests to a veterinary panel, who "award" points depending on the severity of the defect. Ask your local vet to explain the scoring system to you, so that you are fully aware before you go and see the puppies.

Often, the breeder does not own the stud dog, so it may not be possible for you to see him. However, when you do eventually go to see the puppies, make sure you see the bitch as well. If the breeder does not let you see her, *do not buy one of the puppies*. Most breeders are only too happy to let you see their stock, so any reluctance on their part to let you see the mother of the puppy you intend to buy should be viewed with the greatest suspicion.

You should be able to observe the bitch with her pups, when you will have the chance to study her temperament, bearing in mind the important part it plays in the development and character of your chosen pup. It is understandable if she shows some apprehension should you touch her puppies – when you want to start picking them up, the breeder will probably remove her from the room.

If she shows any other displays of nervousness or aggression, please think very carefully before buying one. To see a litter of puppies is a wonderful sight and it is easy to get carried away, letting your heart rule your head and not paying sufficient attention to the character of the bitch. A bad decision at this stage though could mean the beginning of years of trauma and heartache for you and your family.

Assuming that the bitch's temperament is all that it should be and the pups are obviously healthy and well adjusted, you then have to choose one! It is not necessarily a good idea to go for the biggest and boldest pup in the litter. He has become like that by pushing and bullying his brothers and sisters, having found that he gets a bigger share of food and attention that way. Although this need not be a fault, if you do pick this bossy puppy, you must be prepared for him to try that behaviour out on you, so if you are of a gentle and quiet disposition, this pup may not be the right one for you.

In the same way, the quietest pup in the litter will not adapt very easily if you have a noisy home full of boisterous children!

It is very much a matter of personal choice, but do try to use common sense if possible. Personally, I'm a great believer in instinct when it comes to selecting a puppy, but then not everyone's instincts are the right ones!

Medical Ailments

You may have read all the categories previously mentioned, yet still cannot "fit" your dog into any one of them, so cannot understand *why* your dog is being aggressive.

If this is the case, it would be advisable to have your dog thoroughly checked over by your veterinary surgeon. Simple things, such as ear infections, bad teeth, blocked anal glands, etc., can cause your dog to be bad tempered. Once treated, you may find that his aggressive behaviour ceases.

Unfortunately, there are more serious conditions, such as brain tumours, which cause the dog to act irrationally. Obviously in such cases, your vet is the best person qualified to give an opinion as to the dog's future.

Dangerous Dogs

The final category which should be mentioned is the dog that has been specifically bred for fighting, and in some instances is actually *encouraged* to be aggressive. Of these dogs, the most notable is the American Pit Bull Terrier. Following a spate of attacks on people by these dogs, and also, it must be said, by some other breeds, the Dangerous Dogs Act 1991 was brought into force. Hopefully, none of the readers of this book will ever find themselves in possession of a truly vicious dog, but it is as well to know the outline of this Act, so on page 128 I give details of it.

5

KEEPING YOUR DOG HEALTHY

With luck, your dog will lead a long and healthy life. A few sensible precautions on your part will increase the chances of your dog doing just that. You also have a responsibility to ensure that your dog does not spread disease to other dogs or indeed to humans.

Regular Inoculations

With the system currently in operation in this country, killer diseases which can affect dogs have been closely controlled and in some cases almost eradicated.

The most lethal of them all, rabies, has been so far excluded from the UK and Ireland by the quarantine laws. Quarantine means long separation from our dogs, which is not very pleasant, but it is infinitely better than bringing in a disease which could have such awful consequences on domestic animals, wild life and humans.

It is up to all of us to act responsibly to ensure that rabies never reaches this country and to report any known instances of quarantine evasion to the authorities immediately.

The four main diseases which can be controlled by regular inoculation are distemper, hepatitis, leptospirosis and parvo virus. This last disease, parvo virus, is relatively new. It particularly affects young puppies and elderly dogs and is quite virulent in some parts of the country.

All dogs must be inoculated against these diseases, to lessen even further the chance of an epidemic. Puppies are usually inoculated at around eight weeks and again at twelve weeks. After that, yearly booster inoculations are essential, so that the dog has continual protection throughout his life. Until puppies have received their second inoculation at twelve weeks, they should not be mixed with other dogs.

Worming

There are two groups of worms which can affect dogs, namely the nematode group and the cestode group. These are more commonly known as roundworms and tapeworms. Signs of worm infestation in the dog are abnormal hunger, diarrhoea, anal itching, poor growth and loss of condition.

The unwormed dog can pass worms to other dogs, via the worm eggs. The eggs are passed by the dog in his faeces. These eggs are then moved around by the wind, rain and on the soles of people's shoes. The eggs can then adhere to passing dogs, sticking to their feet and coat. The dog can then ingest the eggs when licking himself, thus the life cycle of the egg continues, resulting in worm infestation.

It is also possible for these eggs to be ingested by humans, especially children. By touching infested ground, or by stroking a dog who has the worm eggs attached to his coat and then putting their hands in their mouths, people can ingest the eggs. The cycle of the egg is then altered and in rare circumstances can lead to blindness and mental retardation. This disease is called Visceral Larvae Migrans and is caused by the egg of the roundworm Toxocara Canis.

There is also a strain of tapeworm, which, if ingested during its development stage, can affect humans, causing a disease called Hydatidosis, which affects the liver and lungs. Fortunately, cases of this disease are extremely rare.

All this unpleasantness can be avoided if all dog owners abide by the following simple rules:

1. All puppies should be wormed before leaving the breeder, at three weeks and five weeks of age. They should be wormed again twice more by the time they reach 13 weeks. Thereafter they should be regularly wormed every six months throughout their lives.

2. Bitches who are about to be bred from should be wormed prior to mating and again after the puppies are weaned.

3. All faeces should be removed daily from the garden and burned or hygienically disposed of. Always remove any faeces your dog leaves behind when out on exercise.

4. Always wash your hands after handling your dog, before consuming food.

By following these simple procedures, you can be assured that you have taken all possible steps to prevent your dog passing the infection to other dogs or humans.

Fleas

Dog fleas are quite indiscriminate and will infest the clean, healthy dog just as much as the dirty, neglected animal. The flea lives on the dog, sucking blood, and its bites can cause extreme irritation. Some dogs also become allergic to the saliva which is injected into the skin when the flea bites. As well as the irritation caused, fleas are also the intermediate host of the tapeworm.

Fleas can be seen quickly moving over the dog's skin and are particularly partial to the base of the dog's tail and behind its ears. Flea droppings look like specks of grit and are especially visible on the dog's stomach. Fleas like warmth and will lay their eggs in the gap between the carpet and the skirting board, between the floorboards, in the pile of fitted carpets and in the dog's bedding and basket. After the eggs hatch, the larvae stage can remain dormant for anything up to one year, if the temperature is not warm enough.

The adult fleas spend only a short time actually on the dog, just long enough to feed, mate and then they jump off, either onto the floor, another dog or cat, or, worse still, onto you.

At one time, flea infestations were confined to the warmer summer months, but nowadays, with more and more homes being centrally heated, the larvae can hatch all year round, jumping on to the next passing host, after hatching. Flea spray preparations can be obtained from your vet and regular treatment of the dog, his bedding and all carpet edges, as well as regular use of the vacuum cleaner, will keep the problem at bay.

Exercise

It is impossible to generalise over how much exercise you should give your dog. Some need a five mile walk daily, whilst others only need a short run around the park. As a very rough guide, medium to large breeds such as Alsatians, Retrievers, Labradors, Collies, etc., should have at least one *good* walk every day, supplemented with shorter walks on the lead. The very large heavy breeds, such as Newfoundlands, Pyreneans and St. Bernards, should not be run for miles and miles – they are quite content to have shorter, more sedate regular exercise, although they can walk a fair distance at a gentle pace. With the smaller breeds, it very much depends on the type of dog – some small dogs can run for hours, whilst others can only take exercise in short bursts. Find out from the breeder, or the vet, exactly how much your particular dog should have. With very young puppies, especially those who are going to grow into big dogs, exercise should be very moderate during the first few months, as their young bones are forming all the time and could be damaged through over exercise.

Grooming

Whether your dog has a short or long coat, he should be brushed regularly, to keep his coat healthy, clean and tangle-free. The shorter-coated dog should be brushed at least once a week, whilst the dog with a longer coat needs brushing daily to keep it in tip-top condition. A few minutes spent every day is far better than half an hour once a week. When you are brushing your dog, it is also a good time to check him over and examine him.

Bathing

It is really a personal choice as to how often you bath your dog, but regular brushing should be sufficient most of the time. Obviously, if your dog has rolled in something unpleasant, or during a heavy moult, a bath may be necessary. It is also a good idea to bath a bitch once she has finished her season, to get rid of any "interesting" smells which may remain. On these occasions, do use a proper, good quality dog shampoo and rinse the coat thoroughly.

Where possible, bath your dog on a warm, sunny day,

so that after you have removed the excess water with a towel, your dog can stay outside and dry his coat properly. If it is a cold or wet day, dry as much as possible with a towel, then use a hair drier, or let him lie in front of a warm, but not hot, fire. Make sure that his joints are dried thoroughly, to prevent any future problems with rheumatism.

Swimming

Many dogs enjoy swimming and it can be very good exercise for them. If you do allow your dog into the sea, you must rinse his coat well in fresh water when you return home, as the salt and the sand can cause skin irritation. Also, please be considerate if you take your dog onto the beach. It can be very annoying for other beach users to have a dog running through their possessions and having to avoid the little "piles" which dogs can leave behind them!

Heat Stroke

Most dogs do not enjoy being exposed to hot sun. Their body temperature is higher than ours and their tolerance of heat is lower. During the summer months, it is best to restrict the dog to light exercise during the heat of the day, leaving strenuous exercise either for early morning or evening. Make sure they always have access to both shade and water.

Never leave a dog unattended in a car during warm weather. Even with the windows open, the temperature can soar within minutes, causing the dog extreme distress, which can lead very quickly to collapse and death. I did an experiment with my own car, to see what the temperature was inside, on a hot, sunny day. The car, an estate, was parked on the roadside, with a small amount of shade being cast on it. The outside temperature was 80° Fahrenheit.

With all the windows fully opened, the sunroof and the tailgate open, after ten mintues the temperature inside the car was the same as outside, i.e. 80°.

With the windows half open, the sunroof open and the tailgate shut (as you may possibly leave the car when popping into a shop), within ten minutes the temperature inside the car was 98°.

With windows, sunroof and tailgate all shut, the temperature inside the car reached 122° within ten minutes. So, you can see that even with leaving windows opened, the dog would very quickly be overcome by the heat and lack of air circulation.

However, if you ever come across a dog which is unfortunate enough to suffer from heat stroke, you must take action fast. The signs are panting, profuse salivation, vomiting and general weakness. Quickly move the dog to a cool, airy place and apply cold water and/or ice packs to the head, neck and shoulders and seek veterinary assistance immediately.

Feeding

Nowadays, the choice of what to feed your dog is very extensive, ranging from fresh meat, canned meat, all-in-one dried foods, to various forms of processed food. What you decide upon is basically a personal matter between you and your dog, but don't allow him to become a fussy eater. If he turns his nose up at what you provide, don't immediately rush out and buy something different. Assuming he is not ill and provided that the food is not stale, leave the bowl down for a couple of minutes and if he hasn't eaten it, pick it up again. Try him once more, half an hour later and if he still doesn't eat, remove the bowl, keep the food fresh and give it to him for his next meal. Dogs are not stupid. He will not starve himself. He can actually survive for several days without food, provided he has access to fresh water. Obviously, if your dog has previously been a good, unfussy eater and suddenly goes off his food, something is wrong and you should take him to the vet. This is particularly so with young puppies.

All dogs are different – some gulp their food down ravenously, whilst others pick delicately, taking a long time to clear their dishes. However, if you have the type of dog who will only eat best steak, then that's because *you* have let him choose. After all, I'm sure you'd rather eat steak than fish fingers, given the choice, but cost dictates that you can't!

If you decide to feed your dog fresh meat, give it to him raw and don't waste all the essential vitamins by boiling them out during cooking. You may not like the look of raw meat, but I assure you your dog will – and the taste! In the wild, dogs didn't carry their primus stoves around with them to cook their kill on! Their teeth and stomachs are designed for eating and digesting raw meat, so please, don't cook it.

Don't feed him solely on meat and biscuits. Substitute the biscuit with bran occasionally – particularly if your dog is putting on weight when he shouldn't. Bran is a very good filler and will make him feel replete without putting on unwanted weight. Feed him vegetables too, raw if possible.

If you are having temperament problems with your dog, either with aggression, or hyper-activity, have a look at his diet. There has been some research done, which has shown that a reduction in the protein content of the dog's diet can have a calming effect on such dogs, over a period. Basically, too much protein can over-fuel the dog, in the same way as extra oats charge-up a horse. If you feel your dog fits into one of these categories, try changing to a food high in cereals and feed white meat rather than red – in fact choose a blander diet overall.

Once your dog is past puppyhood and is on a balanced diet, there is no need to give him any liquid other than water to drink. Milk is not necessary and can in fact upset the stomach. Too much milk is also a big factor in dogs becoming overweight.

Don't be tempted to feed your dog "human" food as tit-bits. Chocolate designed for us to eat is not suitable for your dog. It contains refined sugar, which the dog cannot digest. The fact that he will eat it if offered is quite irrelevant – given the chance he'll eat all kinds of things that aren't good for him.

If you must give your dog tit-bits, either buy a proprietary brand of dog treats, or give him apples or a small piece of cheese. Apples contain natural sugar, which the dog can digest and most dogs love cheese, which does no harm in small quantities.

As regards to the amount you should feed, a rough guide is to feed ½ oz of total food per pound of target bodyweight. For example, if your dog should weigh 30 lbs, then he should have no more than 15 oz of total food per day. Like people, dogs have varying metabolic rates and some dogs may get overweight given the average quantity of food per day. With growing puppies, the diet will obviously not be the same as for a full-grown dog – if you have not obtained a diet sheet from the breeder, get advice from your vet. As dogs grow old, their food requirements may change, so again, get advice from the vet.

Castration
Earlier in the book, I briefly touched on the subject of castrating a male dog and the possible outcome of such

action. Apart from the obvious fact that castrated males cannot reproduce, it can, in certain cases, help with behavioural problems. But castration is not the answer to every training problem. It does not stop them forever sniffing the ground, sniffing other dogs or sniffing humans in places that we wish they wouldn't! It will not stop them recognising the difference between male and female dogs and it will not stop them cocking their legs. Neither will it automatically stop them from running off, or attempting to mount bitches.

Having listed the things which castration will probably not help, there are some occasions when it can have positive results. If your dog is very sexually possessive, for example with one particular member of the family, or with a female dog who lives in the same house, and this possessiveness culminates in shows of aggression, then castrating the dog can have beneficial results. It does not work overnight, however, and can take anything up to six months before you see any improvement. You should not rely on the operation to stop the problem on its own and you should train the dog at the same time, preferably with the help of a good training club, so that the combination will produce the required results.

As I mentioned in the opening chapter, injections simulating castration can be tried first, to assess their reaction before taking the step of having your dog operated on.

If you are contemplating having your dog castrated, please wait until he is properly mature. A dog neutered while still a puppy will not develop properly, either physically or mentally. Once you have had him castrated, watch his weight carefully, as the act of castration, which prevents the circulation of the hormone testosterone, can result in an increase of fat, due to a lowered metabolic rate. Any sign of weight increase should be dealt with immediately – too much weight causes numerous health problems and can kill your dog.

Spaying

If you have a female dog, she will come into season roughly twice a year, starting any time after five or six months of age. The term "season" means that, for three to four weeks at a time, her body will go through the process which, if allowed, will culminate in mating and the production of puppies. I know that some people are of the opinion that it does a bitch good to allow her to have a litter. I have not seen any evidence to prove this theory.

In my opinion, unless you have an exceptional specimen of a particular breed and know that you can get good homes for all the puppies, to breed from a bitch, just because it's natural, is very irresponsible. Even worse are those people who breed from their bitch to make money from the sale of the puppies. Dog breeding should be left to the knowledgeable specialist. Indeed, if the laws regarding breeding were tightened up and revolting places like puppy farms and dog supermarkets were closed down, we would see a dramatic reduction in the number of unwanted dogs, pedigree and non-pedigree alike, sitting in rescue centres up and down the country.

Before any bitch is bred from, she should firstly be at least two years old and have had tests to see whether she carries any genetic abnormalities, with the chosen stud dog also tested in the same way. It is the responsibility of the breeder to ensure that all puppies go to a good home and they should also be prepared to take back any puppies who cannot be kept by their new owners.

Dog breeding takes planning – it is not just a case of putting any old bitch to the nearest male dog and letting them do what comes naturally.

So, assuming that you are not going to breed from your

bitch, you have two choices. You can ensure that each time she comes into season, for the entire length of the season, that she is kept away from all male dogs and only exercised on the lead, well away from all other dogs. Or you could put her into kennels each time she has a season, which could prove very costly.

The alternative is to have her spayed – that is to remove her ovaries surgically and in some cases part of the uterus, thus stopping the seasons and making it impossible for her to reproduce. The operation itself is very common and should ideally be done after the bitch has had her first season, preferably mid-way between the end of the first one and the beginning of the second.

You can have her spayed before she ever has a season, but I would strongly advise against this. Although physically possible, I have seen the mental result of bitches being spayed before they have had a season. Many of them get mentally screwed up at around the time when their season would have been due.

The fact that some vets will perform the operation before the bitch has had one season does not, to me, make it right. After all, the vet doesn't have to live with the mental effect that it can have on the bitch. I also like to know that my bitch has developed normally, allowing her to go through the process of one season first, before being spayed.

6

INTRODUCING A SECOND DOG

Nowadays, many families are becoming multi-dog. They start with one, then get another as company for the first one and so on. Normally, second and subsequent dogs join the family without many problems, but there are things which you can do to aid the acceptance process.

Generally speaking, if you already have a male dog, it is better to choose a female as the second dog. There is less risk of fighting between male and female, whereas male dogs can be very territorial and resent another male dog intruding on their territory. Naturally, care must be taken with a male and female dog in the same household when the bitch comes into season, but having her spayed after the first season will resolve that problem. There *is* a slight possibility that once your male dog has a female dog for a companion, he may become a little possessive towards her, by showing aggression to other male dogs who approach his bitch.

Whichever sex you decide upon, try and arrange for their first meeting to be on neutral territory, in case the first dog should show any territorial aggression towards the newcomer. Obviously, if the new dog is a young puppy, you will have to bring the pup straight home, but make sure that the first dog's favourite and most loved member of the family is not the one who carries the puppy indoors. Usually, whatever sex the new puppy is, the original dog will make allowances, and will recognise it as a baby, who offers no threat to his position within the family.

Whether it's a puppy or an older dog, both dogs will adjust more easily if you accept that between them, *they* will work out who is going to be boss dog over the other. Don't try and use human logic by assuming that the dog who was in the house first should be number one dog. It may turn out that way, but if it doesn't and you interfere and upset the natural order of things, you could end up with a very unpleasant situation. By watching their behaviour towards one another, you will quickly see which dog is showing signs of subservience. The underdog will possibly lie down when the other approaches and sniffs him. He may allow the other dog to take his food – here you *should* interfere, by feeding the two dogs separately, or you will end up with one very overweight dog! Boss dog will demonstrate his superiority by pushing the other out of the way when affection is in the offing. He will always try to be first out of the door when going for walks and first into the car when going for a ride. He may well threaten the other dog verbally, to instil his dominance.

Don't try to treat the two dogs as equals – in their world equality does not exist, remember their basic instincts. Once the pecking order has been established, don't be tempted to compensate the underdog by cuddling him more than the boss dog, or feeding him an extra tit-bit. This will merely antagonise the boss dog, who will then punish his subordinate for what he considers to be liberty-taking and getting above his position.

Always allow boss dog to be first through the door, after you. Feed him first, welcome him first when you come in. You are not showing favouritism by doing this –

you're simply accepting the natural order which both dogs recognise.

If you have an elderly dog and are bringing a young puppy into the household, you must obviously take care that the boisterous behaviour of the youngster does not harm the old dog. The youngster will obviously want to play and here you can shield the older dog a little, by getting on to the floor and playing with the pup yourself, to deflect unwanted attention away from the older one. Having said that, don't interfere when the older dog tells the puppy off. He must be allowed to put the pup in his place, or the youngster could make the older dog's life a misery.

Very often, you find that bringing a young puppy into the household can revitalise the older dog, so don't worry too much, just be sensible.

Whilst on the subject of having second and subsequent dogs, please don't be tempted to get two puppies together, as this can have disastrous consequences. I have a friend who says that "puppy plus puppy equals puppy squared" and it will certainly feel like that at times – two puppies together can wreak the havoc of four!

Firstly, the puppies will always relate to one another, before you, especially if they are litter brothers or sisters, as they will have been together since birth. Two puppies living together will form an attachment that is far more important to them than any human attachment. They will gang-up, as together they are a pack. Because they are a pack, they may become aggressive to other, single dogs.

If one is a chewer, he will influence the non-chewer, not the other way around. They will compete with one another at every opportunity. Walking on the lead will turn into a race, as will getting out of the front door, getting to their food, etc. If one is a barker, he will encourage the other to bark. Having two together will lead you to lump them together, rather than letting their individual characters emerge. When it comes to house training, the slower of the two to become clean will influence the other into being dirty again.

I could cite many more examples of why having two puppies together could be a dreadful combination. If you feel that I am coming strong on this subject, it is because many years ago, I did exactly what I'm trying to deter you from doing. I obtained two dear little cross-bred puppies – I just couldn't separate them – and the ensuing round of catastrophies led me to joining a dog training club and getting hooked on dog training! I would add that both dogs lived to a grand age, but not before they had made a good job of trying to wreck each other, my home and my nerves! Since then, I have met many people who have made the same mistake and were pulling their hair out over the antics of their puppies. So, if it is your intention to go and get two puppies, please think again. Get one first, let him reach maturity, then go and get the second.

Full Circle

So, you've just brought your second dog home. Turn back to the beginning of the book . . .

INDEX

The Dangerous Dogs Act 1991

The Act states that any dog of the type known as the Pit Bull Terrier, any dog of the type known as the Japanese Tosa, and any dog being of a type appearing to have been bred for fighting, *must*:

Not be bred from.
Not be sold, exchanged, advertised for sale or given as a gift.
Not be abandoned, or allowed to stray.
When in a public place be muzzled and held on a lead.
Be securely held by a person over sixteen years of age.

Penalties for disobeying the above may include any, or all of the following:

The dog would be destroyed.
The owner would be liable for a fine, or a term of imprisonment, or both.
The owner may be disqualified from keeping a dog, for such a period as the court deems fit.

The Act can also be enforced against *any* breed of dog which is deemed to be dangerously out of control in a public place. Even if the dog has not injured anyone, if there are grounds for reasonable apprehension that it may do so, the Act allows for all or any of the restrictions to be enforced.

There are some dogs, bred from "fighting" stock, but owned by responsible people, who keep the dog simply as a pet and never allow it to develop aggressive tendencies. It is most unfortunate that these owners are penalized, because of the actions of others. However, as the Act stands, all owners of the breeds mentioned must comply with its rules. Likewise, *all* dog owners must be diligent and act responsibly, to ensure that the actions of their dogs are not misunderstood or misinterpreted.